BUSINESS NEGOTIATING BASICS

Peter Economy

IRWIN
Professional Publishing
Burr Ridge, Illinois
New York, New York

The Briefcase Books Series

Research shows that people who buy business books (1) want books that can be read quickly, perhaps on a plane trip, commuting on a train, or overnight, and (2) feel their time and money were well spent if they get two or three useful insights or techniques for improving their professional skills or helping them with a current problem at work.

Briefcase Books were designed to meet these two criteria. They focus on necessary skills and problem areas, and include real-world examples from practicing managers and professionals. Inside these books you'll find useful, practical information and techniques in a straightforward, concise, and easy-to-read format.

This book and others like it in the Briefcase Books series can quickly give you insights and answers regarding your current needs and problems. And they are useful references for future situations and problems.

If you find this book or any other in this series to be of value, please share it with your coworkers. With tens of thousands of new books published each year, any book that can simplify the growing complexities in managing others needs to be circulated as widely as possible.

Robert B. Nelson
Series Editor

© RICHARD D. IRWIN, INC., 1994

Sponsoring editor: Cynthia A. Zigmund
Project editor: Rebecca Dodson
Production manager: Jon Christopher
Designer: Laurie Entringer
Compositor: William C. Brown
Typeface: 11/13 Palatino
Printer: The Book Press, Inc.

Library of Congress Cataloging-in-Publication Data

Economy, Peter.
    Business negotiating basics/Peter Economy.
        p.   cm.—(The Briefcase books series)
        ISBN 1–55623–841–X   ISE: 0–7863–0202–X
        1. Negotiation in business.   I. Title.   II. Series.
    HD58.6.E26 1994
    658.4—dc20   93–11510

Printed in the United States of America
1   2   3   4   5   6   7   8   9   0   BP   9   8   7   6   5   4   3   2

To my son Peter J—wondrous child of light.

Foreword

My mission in life has been to be a conveyor of simple truths. It is for that reason that I'm pleased to be able to introduce The Briefcase Books Series, which seeks to provide simple, practical, and direct answers to the most common problems managers face on a daily basis.

It has been my experience that, in the field of business, common sense is not common practice. It is refreshing to find a series of books that glorifies common sense in dealing with people in the workplace.

Take the skill of listening. We all know that it is important to listen, yet how many of us actually do it well? I suggest it would be rare to find one in a hundred managers who is truly a good listener. Most people focus on what they are going to say next when someone else is talking. They would seldom if ever think to check what they thought they heard to make sure it is accurate. And they seldom acknowledge or attempt to deal with emotions whey they occur in speaking with someone at work. These are basic errors in the use of this basic skill. And regardless of how much education or experience you have, you should know how to listen.

But how much training have you had on the topic of listening? Have you ever had a course on the topic? Have you ever tested your ability to listen? Have you ever discussed with others how you could listen better with greater comprehension and respect? Probably not—even though this fundamental interpersonal skill could cripple the most talented individual if he or she is not good at it.

Fortunately, listening is just one of the fundamental skills singled out for its own volume in The Briefcase Books Series. Others include books on making presentations, negotiating, problem-solving, and handling stress. And other volumes are planned even as I write this.

The Briefcase Books Series focuses on those basic skills that managers must master to excel at work. Whether you are new to managing or are a seasoned manager, you'll find these books of value in obtaining useful insights and fundamental knowledge you can use for your entire career.

Ken Blanchard
Co-author, *The One-Minute Manager*

Preface

While the techniques and principles presented in this book are of direct benefit to almost anyone in business, *Business Negotiating Basics* was written especially for those professionals, managers, supervisors, and others who, as a normal part of their jobs, interface with vendors or other outside resources, or who work closely with co-workers to get their jobs done.

The reader will immediately and directly benefit through application of the skills presented in the chapters that follow. Few of us are conversant with the full range of basic business negotiation skills. Furthermore, most of us lack a unified approach to negotiation. *Business Negotiating Basics* presents a complete system of business negotiation skills and techniques that can be quickly and effectively applied to your unique circumstances.

This system consists of three key parts—the seven basic steps of business negotiation, a comprehensive guide to identifying and countering common negotiation tactics and strategies, and the PREP model of negotiation preparation. By applying the techniques presented in *Business Negotiating Basics*, you will build a firm foundation of negotiation skills that you can rely on day after day.

The concepts presented here have direct application in any business—whether high-tech or low-tech, small or large, private or public, service or manufacturing. Furthermore, the techniques outlined can be easily grasped and applied by anyone at any level within your organization.

Many books on the market address the subject of negotiation—you have undoubtedly seen or read many of
them by now. Whether they implore you to win by intimidation or attempt to sell you on the idea of negotiation
as an art, the majority of negotiation books fail to address
the basic everyday needs of American businesspeople.
This is because the vast majority of negotiation books concentrate primarily on the universe of buying or selling
transactions.

Business Negotiating Basics shows that the full range of
business negotiation extends well beyond the boundaries
of buying and selling transactions. Indeed, the word *negotiate* is derived from the Latin word *negotiari,* to carry
on business. And, as we all know, there is a lot more to
carrying on business than just agreeing to a price with one
of your suppliers.

In business, as well as in everyday life, you are constantly involved in situations that require the application
of negotiation skills. Think about the last time that you
tried to obtain some new office furniture. Do you recall
the back-and-forth, "give-and-take" process you went
through to get your request approved? If you are like me,
you used a mixture of persuasion, experience, cajoling,
and horse trading to get your request approved. As you
can see, even the most basic business task can be primarily a negotiation.

Most businesspeople negotiate far more often than they
realize. After reading this book, you will have a much
better sense of the nature of everyday business negotiations. You will discover that, instead of being isolated in-
cidents, negotiations are being conducted all the time—
by yourself and by your co-workers and other business
associates.

You can improve your business skills by applying the basics outlined in this book. This system has worked for me—I know it will work for you. If you have any questions, I would be happy to personally address them. Please write to me in care of the publisher. Best wishes.

Peter Economy
Pacific Beach, California

Acknowledgments

Thanks to Severo Esquivel, Cathy Lexin, and Tim Sturtevant for their trust and confidence in me; Debbie Fritsch for her uncanny business acumen and continuing advice; Pat Boyce, who successfully compressed a lifetime of priceless business experience into six short years, for which I am forever grateful; Bill Vancanagan at Datsopoulos, MacDonald, and Lind for his insightful legal perspectives; Winifred Golden for her ongoing support; Gary Ales for his practical lessons in real-life negotiations; Zanzibar for countless double espresso mochas; John Adams for many late nights with *Nixon in China*; Anna Diaz for Ducky; Kate Bush for getting me through 1992 (I just knew something good was going to happen); Susan Brehm for periodic and timely reality checks; Lee Hill for his perspectives on alternate thought processes; Robert Nelson for his ongoing literary support and eternal friendship; and my wife Jan for love and kisses and beautiful children.

Contents

Chapter One

Why Negotiate?

It is the nature of men to be bound by the benefits they confer as much as by those they receive.

Niccolò Machiavelli

Why read another book about negotiation? The answer is simple: whether you realize it or not, you are already a negotiator. In fact, it's very likely that you spend more time negotiating with your co-workers, customers, and other business associates than you allocate to any other specific task that you perform as a part of your everyday business. The question then becomes: "How good a negotiator are you?"

You may view negotiators only in the context of world diplomacy—spending months arguing about the shape or length of the negotiating table. Perhaps your idea of a negotiator is the aggressive labor arbitrator who tries to pull union and management positions into conjunction long enough to keep a steel or auto plant functioning and strike free for a couple more years. Or, you may picture the majority of negotiators as deal-makers who get their way by bullying their opponents into submission.

While these people are all indeed negotiators, professional ones at that, they are only the visible tip of the enormous, mostly submerged iceberg that consists of all businesspeople. Conflict, negotiation, cooperation, and, ultimately, consensus are the lifeblood of business. We all negotiate—on a daily, hourly, and, yes, even on a minute-to-minute basis at times. We are all catalysts in the business process.

CONFLICT AND CONSENSUS

As a business professional, you get paid to make things happen. How do you get things done? There are three basic methods you can use to accomplish a business goal:

1. Do it yourself.
2. Have someone else do it.
3. Work with someone else to get it done.

Depending on the situation, you must decide which of these options will ensure that you reach your desired goal.

The first method, doing it yourself, requires little or no negotiation with others. While you may go through an extensive process of internal negotiation to decide the best approach to a problem, and you may solicit the advice of your co-workers, the actual work process is performed by only one person. Individually, however, you can achieve only a limited quantity of work. You are much more effective when given the opportunity, you delegate tasks to others. Successful managers delegate as much of their work as possible.

Once another person enters into your plan for goal attainment, you have set the stage for negotiation. When you delegate tasks to another individual, you include the deadline or schedule, and the expected standards of quality. You delegate tasks to an employee through a give-and-take process of cooperative negotiation leading to a final agreement on what exactly will be provided, including, if needed, any rearrangement of priorities among other projects.

In the following example, note the interplay of give-and-take between the parties as a task is delegated:

* * * * *

"Tony, please see me as soon as you have the opportunity."

"I'll be right there, Cathy."

"I have decided to assign an important project to you, Tony. Are you familiar with the time-phased budget that we drew up last month on the aircraft mission planning software project?"

"You bet. I helped Pam put some of the numbers together."

"As you know, Pam has been promoted out of our department. I need a revised budget as soon as possible. Our programming effort is falling behind and the milestones are starting to slip."

"How soon do you need it?"

"I know this is short notice, but I need the revised budget in time to present to the weekly management meeting tomorrow morning at 9:00."

"Wow—that's going to be a tough schedule to meet. I'm working on the quarterly program right now with Marty. We're supposed to have the first run in hard copy before the close of business today."

"The pro forma can wait. Who else is familiar with the spreadsheets besides Marty and yourself?"

"I think that Anna has worked with them before."

"Fine, Tony, here's the plan. I'll get together with Anna's supervisor and see if we can't get Anna to work with Marty on the quarterly pro forma. I want you to get started on the mission planning software budget right away. I'll have Anna come and see you. You can bring her up to speed on the quarterly financials so she'll be able to jump right in on them. Any questions?"

* * * * *

Effective delegation only occurs in the presence of effective negotiation. The interdependence of delegation and negotiation is such a natural part of our business lives that many of us may not even notice it. The ability to delegate skillfully, however, forms the bedrock upon which we build much of our effectiveness in business.

THE IMPORTANCE OF WIN-WIN NEGOTIATING

We all want to win. Not only is it our job to win but, with the conditioning that we have received as a result of our rugged-individualist American traditions, most of us are constantly and unconsciously driven to win.

Regardless of your job title, it is likely that your success at work is measured in terms of winning. You finally signed the account that you have been chasing for the last three years. You were successful in getting a key supplier to drop his price. You got the union to back off on its demands for a cost-of-living increase. You just made your sales quota for the month. Your department met its production goals for the year.

In the United States, the spotlight tends to focus on those people who have achieved the greatest success. It is not important that this success may have been achieved at tremendous expense to another party, or that long-term relationships have been sacrificed to gain a short-term advantage. The business environment in which we work pushes us to seek every possible opportunity to win—regardless of the consequences to those around us. As a result, some of us are so driven to win that we will compromise our personal ethics or even break the law to be successful.

The best businesspeople, and the best negotiators, are those who are driven to win, but not at the expense of their co-workers, their clients, their customers, or their counterparts. Instead, the truly successful business negotiator realizes that the best outcome is one that creates winners on both sides of the agreement.

This is the essence of win-win negotiating. There is nothing wrong with being a winner. However, there is most definitely something wrong with winning at the expense of your counterpart. In win-win negotiation, all parties to the negotiation achieve their goals. Your goal may be to get the best price possible. Your vendor's goal may be to lock you into a long-term sales contract. In a win-win outcome, both goals will be met, and both parties to the agreement will be satisfied as a result.

The old style of negotiation emphasized the win-lose school of thought. Win through intimidation. Use your power, or the power of your corporation, to force your opponents into submission. Refuse to compromise your positions or to consider alternatives. In win-lose negotiation, one party achieves its goals, while the other party doesn't.

A win-lose outcome might work fine for the winning party—at least in the short-term. However, over the long term, win-lose outcomes are fundamentally flawed. When you create a loser, you also create an opponent. At a minimum, you can expect your opponent to harbor a deep resentment for being forced into such an unenviable position. At worst, your newfound opponent may dedicate his or her entire career to crushing you or your organization.

It's relatively easy to negotiate a win-lose outcome—especially if you have some sort of advantage that you can use as leverage against your opponent. It's a much greater challenge to create and negotiate win-win solutions. Win-win solutions are the result of flexibility, creativity, and teamwork on the part of both parties. Win-win solutions can only be achieved when both parties are sincerely interested in discovering the needs, goals, and interests of their counterparts. Finally, win-win solutions demand a firm commitment to the concepts of equity and fair play.

Dedicate yourself to being a win-win negotiator. Explore alternatives and the widest possible range of solutions with your counterpart. Refuse to follow the path of least resistance and force a win-lose outcome on the other party. While a win-lose outcome may address your immediate needs or solve your immediate problems, it is guaranteed to sabotage your long-term goals.

EVERYDAY BUSINESS NEGOTIATIONS

The word "negotiate" is defined by *Webster's New World Dictionary* as "to confer, bargain, or discuss with a view to reaching agreement." Clearly, many business situations meet that definition. The key word is agreement. The whole purpose of negotiation is to reach an agreement. To further illustrate the many different kinds of negotiations that we may become involved in, several examples are listed below. This list is by no means exhaustive. There are undoubtedly many others that are unique to your particular business environment.

Inside the Organization

❏ To obtain a pay raise.
❏ To implement a new idea.
❏ To make an exception to company policy.
❏ To obtain more time to complete a project.
❏ To be assigned greater responsibilities.

Outside the Organization

❏ To improve service.
❏ To place an order.
❏ To change specifications.

- ❑ To discuss pending price increases.
- ❑ To modify delivery dates.
- ❑ To schedule a sales meeting with a big client.

Think about the many different situations in which you negotiate. Not a single business day goes by without your having to negotiate with someone about something— even if it's just to decide where to have lunch, and who is going to pick up the tab.

MULTIPLYING YOUR EFFECTIVENESS

Since so much of your success in business is dependent on eliciting the cooperation of others, one of the easiest ways to multiply your business effectiveness is to improve your negotiation skills. Similarly, one of the easiest ways to diminish your business effectiveness is to mishandle a negotiation with a co-worker, customer, or client due to inadequate skills or misguided motivations.

The next example illustrates the wrong way to negotiate in business. This situation happened to me a few years ago—of course, the names of the other parties have been changed. To this day, I still get a little hot under the collar when I think about it!

* * * * *

"Peter, I spoke to the contracting officer at Robins Air Force Base. See me in my office right away!"

As I hung up the phone, I wondered what could have happened that would cause my boss, Tom, to pull me out of the company's end-of-the-government-fiscal-year party. It was Friday afternoon, September 28.

I knew that we were the apparent low bidder on a computer services contract for the Air Force, but Tom had told me earlier in the day that, since Congress hadn't appropriated any money for the upcoming fiscal year, the contract would be delayed several weeks. Based on that information, I instructed my area supervisor, Joan, to get an early start on her weekend, and I immersed myself in celebrating our company's success.

"What's up, Tom?"

"I just got off the phone with Myrtle, our Robins contracting officer. She's faxing us a copy of a contract for computer services. It looks like we won the competition."

"That's great! So when do we start?"

"Well, that's what I want to talk to you about, Peter. We have to have our staff in place by 9 A.M. Monday morning, October 1."

"You can't be serious! We have to hire seven new employees to staff the project. We haven't even interviewed any candidates yet!"

Although I was vaguely familiar with the proposed scope of the work, my boss Tom had submitted the proposal to the Air Force without my review or input. Our company had fallen on hard times, and Tom was sending out at least two or three new proposals every week. Since our success rate was so low, I didn't bother to read the proposals until Tom alerted me that we were poised for a contract award.

The proposed work was low-tech in nature, but I knew that it would be extremely difficult to recruit candidates, interview them, make employment offers, and get all the Air Force-required security passes, computer access codes, and clearances in place to start work by the first thing Monday morning. In fact, I thought the task to be impossible in such a short time—especially with my limited experience in project start-ups.

I was glad that I would have the benefit of Tom's decades of experience in the government service business. He had been through this many times before. He knew just what to do.

"So where do I start, Tom?"

"I'm sorry, Peter, but you're on your own on this one. I've got to catch a plane in an hour. My wife and I are going to spend the weekend in San Francisco. I suggest that you call Joan right away and get her on a plane to Macon, Georgia, tonight."

"But Joan has already made plans to spend the weekend at the lake with her family."

"That's too bad—she'll just have to cancel her plans. It's your responsibility to have the staff hired and at their workstations at 9 A.M. on Monday. The Air Force can terminate the contract for default if our staff isn't ready to go first thing Monday morning. You'd better get going right away!"

* * * * *

This is a classic example of the win-lose style of negotiation. While Tom achieved his short-term goal of getting the project staffed by 9 A.M. Monday morning (yes, Joan and I *did* manage to pull it together in time), he failed in his long-term goals.

By refusing to change his own plans for the weekend while requiring his staff to change their plans, and by abandoning his staff to work out all the details even though he was the one individual most intimately familiar with the project, Tom created enormous ill will— both towards himself, and towards the company that he owned.

When Tom's staff lost, Tom lost, too. He may have thought he had won—indeed, he could point to his success in getting the project started on schedule. But Tom really lost. Tom lost the trust of his employees. He set a standard that he himself was not willing to follow.

There is really no such thing as a win-lose outcome— at least not in a long-term sense. If a negotiation results in a winner and a loser, then, ultimately, both parties lose. The loser will find a way to be the winner next time— usually at great expense to the party who won the first time around.

Let's see what Tom could have done to create a win-win situation for himself and his staff:

* * * * *

"So where do I start, Tom?"

"I know this is all new to you, Peter. Since this is your first start-up, and in view of the critical time lines, I'm going to be here to walk you through the process this weekend."

"But don't you have vacation plans?"

"I did, but that was before I got the call from Robins Air Force Base. Why don't you get us together with Joan and our recruiter on a conference call within the hour—we're going to have to work together to pull this off on schedule."

* * * * *

Throughout the rest of this book, you will find many more examples to illustrate how the use of the basics of business negotiation will make you more effective in your working life. If you are already using some of these techniques, you will testify to their effectiveness. If, however, you are not presently using these basic business negotiation techniques, you will experience immediate improvement as you begin to apply these new skills.

The key to success is to make everyone a winner whenever you negotiate. Think long-term relationships and solutions, not short-term gains or fixes. Cooperate to identify common goals and negotiate mutually beneficial agreements. Be flexible. Consider the needs of the other party. By following these basic guidelines, you will be able to multiply your effectiveness many times over.

TRUST AND CONFIDENCE

Business is built on a foundation of trust. The most successful businesspeople are those who have developed long-term and deep relationships with their customers, co-workers, and other business contacts. Not only do they promote the development of trust in their daily business relationships, but they also foster the growth of trust in their business units and within the organization as a whole.

Trust is the glue that holds business relationships together over the long term. Without trust, even the best organization will fragment into countless individuals and units, each looking out for its own good and ignoring the needs of the company as a whole.

Some might suggest that determining whether a relationship is long- or short-term will determine how you should approach a negotiation. Indeed, if you expect the business interaction to be short-term, you might be much less flexible in your dealings than you would be in a long-term business relationship.

I personally believe that all business relationships should be considered long-term, and that the development and maintenance of trust is just as important in short-term associations as it is in long-term associations. Short-term relationships often become long-term ones. I have seen far too many bridges burned by businesspeople who, thinking they would never have to deal with a particular person or company again, thought they could take unfair advantage of a situation to their immediate benefit. All too often, the burned bridges we leave behind become significant, lost opportunities in our future business dealings.

Trust is nurtured by commitment. Most people will initially give you the benefit of the doubt when you commit to perform some task within specified parameters. As commitments are honored, trust begins to develop. Trust builds as positive events continue to multiply. The objective difference between the best and worst businesspeople can often be measured simply by observing whether they follow through on their promises. Those who don't often find themselves left out in the cold by their clients, customers, and co-workers.

Let's say that your company has committed to deliver some product to a major customer on a highly defined schedule. The product represents a significant potential profit to your firm. A key component cannot be produced in your current manufacturing facilities. The component is highly specialized, and only a few vendors produce it.

What would you do? Would you choose a vendor who is willing to offer a lower price (thus increasing your margin), but who is consistently late with delivery and has a habit of asking for price increases at the last minute?

Or would you select a vendor who has developed a long-standing relationship with your company? A vendor who consistently honors delivery schedules and holds its pricing? Utilizing this vendor decreases your margin, but at least you can sleep at night knowing your product will be delivered on time.

You can't buy trust, but you can build it. In business, you must do all you can to develop trust with everyone you deal with. Only commit to those things that you are willing to follow through on. Once you have made a commitment, do everything in your power to honor it.

SOURCES OF COMPETITION

There are many sources of competition and, ultimately, conflict. Some sources of competition may be within the company itself, such as the struggle for budgetary or other resources. Others may be external to the organization. Ultimately, much of this competition is merely a reflection of the conflict between our needs and the needs of others.

The drive to succeed is what compelled most managers to get into management in the first place. This goal of success in our personal and business lives often puts us in direct conflict with other people in our organizations.

Every organization has finite resources. This fact leads to the imposition of limits on such things as staffing, travel, training, capital equipment, or anything else that we require to get our work done. In every business, there is invariably active and heated competition to get a fair share of these scarce, but essential, resources.

The sources of conflict and competition are all around us. They are an everyday fact of life. We must be prepared to deal with these business realities and bring them to co-operative resolution as they arise. The following chapters present an approach to the negotiation process that will allow you to easily and effectively resolve conflict and competition with your co-workers, and reach agreement on mutual goals.

Find ways to see beyond the clouds of conflict and competition. Constantly seek out cooperative solutions to business problems. Ultimately, it is only through the co-operative negotiation process that any reliable long-term solution will be found.

COMMUNICATION

From the time we are born, we communicate our needs to the outside world. When we are very young, our requests are often answered with immediate compliance. As we get older, we find that it becomes increasingly necessary to obtain the agreement of others to get action on our requests. Negotiation can help us turn our needs into concrete action.

Negotiation turns the manifestation of your needs into a give-and-take process by which you make your requests and then interact with others to fulfill them. At the same time, your counterpart may make demands of you as a precondition to acceding to your requests.

Communication is the heart of negotiations. If you cannot accurately and effectively communicate your needs, it will be almost impossible for you to achieve your desired goals. Conversely, if the other parties have not effectively communicated their needs to you, they too will have great difficulty in achieving their goals. Clearly, effective communication is essential for the successful care and maintenance of the negotiation process.

WORKSHEETS

To get the most out this book, it can be very beneficial for
you to identify your everyday negotiation situations.
After completing the questionnaire, you may be surprised
to see just how much time you spend negotiating with
your co-workers, customers, and vendors.

What are your primary job responsibilities?

_____

_____

_____

_____

**Which of these responsibilities do you delegate to
others?**

_____

_____

_____

_____

Who do you delegate these responsibilities to?

_____

_____

_____

_____

What tasks do others in your organization delegate to you?

_____

_____

_____

_____

List any contacts you have had with external customers or vendors.

_____

_____

_____

_____

List your specific job duties that require negotiation or compromise.

_____

_____

_____

_____

What kinds of situations require you to negotiate outside of work?

_____

_____

_____

_____

Chapter Two

The Basic Steps

What is easy and obvious is never valued; and what is in itself difficult, if we come to the knowledge of it without difficulty, and without any stretch of thought or judgment, is but little regarded.

David Hume

Now that I have convinced you that negotiation is a significant part of your job, how can *you* become a better negotiator? You have already taken the first step by recognizing that, to be successful in business, you have to be an effective negotiator. Armed with that realization, you're ready to embark on the next step.

The most effective negotiators can see all sides of an issue; the least effective are those who can't see beyond the expediency of their own self-serving positions. The following seven basic steps, discussed in detail in this chapter, are essential to an effective negotiator. Follow these steps, and you will be able to achieve your goals in any kind of business negotiation situation. Ignore them, and it is likely that the result will be a win-lose outcome—with you as the loser.

❑ Be prepared.

❑ Maximize your alternatives.

❑ Negotiate with the right person.
❑ Give yourself room to maneuver.
❑ Don't give away too much too soon.
❑ Be prepared to say no.
❑ Make your word your bond.

The basic skills presented in this chapter are the result of many years of evolution in the theory and practice of business negotiation. Separately, each is a complete, stand-alone skill or technique that, properly applied, will make a significant, positive difference in your negotiations.

However, by utilizing all the steps in a unified and co-ordinated system, you will be able to form a creative partnership with the other party. You will be able to seek, defend, and attain your own goals, while helping your counterparts to attain their goals.

Don't be afraid to make mistakes. In a negotiation, there is really no such thing as a mistake. Every aspect of an agreement can go through many iterations before final agreement is reached. No position has to be forever cast in concrete. Push the envelope. Be willing to get on the edge and test the limits of an agreement. You will value most the agreements that required the most creative use of all of your negotiating skills.

THE FIRST STEP: BE PREPARED

Preparation is undoubtedly the most critical element in any successful business negotiation. I so fervently believe that preparation is essential to ultimate success that I developed the PREP system solely to address this crucial area. The PREP system is discussed in Chapter Four.

Your success in a negotiation will be directly proportional to the amount of preparation that you are willing to undertake before you start. Inadequate preparation will make achievement of your goals very difficult, at best. Sure, you might occasionally get lucky and be able to recover from a lack of preparation. But, to ensure consistently favorable results, you simply must be prepared.

At a minimum, you must familiarize yourself with the background and the history of the situation. Become as knowledgeable as possible about the issues or topics to be discussed. Research them thoroughly. Anticipate your counterpart's interests, goals, and desires. Anticipate his or her rationale. How will you respond to his arguments? How will she respond to yours?

While it's nearly impossible to anticipate the entire universe of the other party's possible goals, interests, and negotiation approaches, you have got to make every effort to anticipate as many of your counterpart's positions as possible if you are going to effectively support your position and efficiently consider your mutual interests.

What can you do to prepare? For starters, you can talk to others in your company who have dealt with this person and try to find out how similar situations were handled in the past. Find copies of correspondence or other documentation that have reduced prior agreements to writing. Talk to co-workers. Network with your associates. Read the local newspapers. Get input from your customers. There is a very high probability that you know someone who has been in a similar situation with the same party. Why waste time reinventing the wheel?

If you are dealing with another company, read their annual reports, marketing brochures, and catalogs. Get an idea of where the other party is coming from, and where he wants to go. Business magazine articles can provide invaluable insights into the other party's motivations. You may, for example, find out that a company that has a history of supplier loyalty is considering new sources for spare parts. Where normally the motivation would be nonexistent, your counterpart may be very motivated to work with you as a new source.

All information is of value. What appears at first glance to be trivial may make or break your agreement.

If you have let yourself enter a negotiation unprepared and you find yourself at a significant disadvantage, get out! You don't have to feel compelled to continue until you have fully prepared yourself and researched all the alternatives and options. It's possible that the other party will recognize your lack of preparation and exert considerable pressure on you. Resist this pressure at all costs, and do not allow yourself to fall prey to this tactic!

What are the potential risks of not being prepared?

❑ Inability to defend your goals.

❑ Shortsightedness in evaluating all the issues.

❑ Succumbing to pressure to close the negotiation.

❑ Giving up too much too soon.

❑ Forgetting key details.

❑ Not considering all alternatives.

❑ Losing control of the negotiation process.

Preparation is the key to successful negotiation. Every hour—no, every minute—that you put into preparation will be rewarded many times over as you proceed. Whenever possible, be prepared and comfortable with all of the facts before you proceed. Understand that, in the fast-paced world of business, there will always be situations where you will have to respond quickly and without the benefit of thorough preparation. However, preparation will help you to control the situation and thereby maximize your success.

THE SECOND STEP: MAXIMIZE
YOUR ALTERNATIVES

If achieving our goals, whatever they may be, is the reason that we negotiate, then options and alternatives are the lifeblood of a negotiation. As the level of complexity of a negotiation increases, so too does the need for creating alternatives and options.

Even the most experienced businesspeople occasionally hit a brick wall or stumbling block in dealings with their associates. How are you going to get around these obstacles to reach your final destination? You will significantly increase your chances if you create more ways to get there.

In any situation, there can be many different approaches to the solution. You may try one approach and find that path blocked. If you are persistent and creative, however, you will eventually find the path that will lead you to success. Don't let yourself be derailed by an initial rebuke. Instead, try another option or alternative. It may be the one that does the trick. If it doesn't, try another. Keep trying until you have explored all possible options.

Be persistent! Have you ever watched an ant carry an object that was seemingly 10 or 20 times larger than the ant itself? The ant might stumble on its way back to its nest but, each time the ant stumbles, it finds another hold on the object, picks it up, and continues towards its goal. Be an ant. Don't let minor setbacks block the way to your own goals. Remember—one of the best ways to reach your goals is to help your counterparts reach their goals.

THE THIRD STEP: NEGOTIATE WITH THE RIGHT PERSON

What do you do if you've repeatedly tried to resolve an issue, but it seems that you're getting nowhere? Maybe your counterpart listens to your proposals, but is not willing to make a decision without obtaining the permission of a superior. Or, even worse, maybe your counterpart agrees to certain terms or conditions, but, after consulting with a supervisor, has to renege. In each of these examples, you can invest a lot of time trying to work out a solution only to find out that the other party doesn't have the authority to reach final agreement with you.

It can be a very frustrating experience to invest hours and hours in a negotiation only to find that you have to present your position again to someone else. It can be a tremendous waste of your precious time. And, as all of us in business know, time definitely is money.

Don't let yourself fall into this trap. Ask very pointed questions. What are the limits of your counterpart's authority? What kinds of decisions can he or she make? What are the limits of those decisions? Does your counterpart really have the authority to bind the company in writing to the agreement that you are about to reach? Will someone else in the organization have to ratify the agreement? If so, how long will that take?

Be alert, however, to the fact that there will be times when a decision-maker will delegate preliminary negotiations to a subordinate. This situation most often occurs when the decision-maker is seeking additional information with which to assess your position, or wants to test your limits. Be polite, but make it clear to the subordinate that the discussions are preliminary, and that the exact details of a final agreement will be settled directly with his or her boss. Be sure to leave plenty of room in your preliminary discussions to negotiate a final agreement.

Don't assume that an imposing title implies real authority to reach a final agreement. Many businesses, for example, grant the title "vice president" to all of their managers.

Others grant such titles in lieu of substantive pay or benefit increases. Some businesses have literally hundreds of vice presidents, many of whom do not have the authority to bind their companies to agreements. Always look beyond titles and make sure the person you are dealing with has real authority.

Authority must be established and understood. You are both wasting precious time if either one of you doesn't have the authority to conclude an agreement. Stand your ground. Refuse to be bullied, snowballed, or stonewalled. Deal with decision-makers.

Always make it a priority to determine early on whether the person you are dealing with has the authority to follow up words with action. You'll be doing yourself a huge favor.

THE FOURTH STEP: GIVE YOURSELF ROOM TO MANEUVER!

Every professional negotiator knows that, in order to reach your goals, you need room to negotiate. This means that you should always ask for more than the minimum you are willing to accept. Most people feel that they have been shortchanged if the other party hasn't had to sacrifice something to reach an agreement.

The problem is this: If your initial position is the one you expect to agree to at the end of your negotiation, then you will not be able to give up any part of that position. If you cannot give up anything, the other party will feel somehow shortchanged. To avoid feeling cheated, he may avoid reaching a final agreement. Even if he does agree, he may feel that he has lost and you have won. This kind of result is definitely not in the interest of either party.

It is therefore *always* in your best interest to leave room to negotiate. Prepare as many alternatives as you can. Be prepared to offer them to the other party, and then be ready to give them away as a part of the negotiation process. Assume that the other party will be doing the same thing. Through this exchange of values, both parties will ultimately be satisfied with the final results.

If you don't leave room to negotiate, your positional inflexibility *will* spill over to the other participant in the negotiation, inducing inflexibility in his positions as he begins to doubt your sincerity. The spiral of inflexibility will inevitably bring the negotiation to a screeching halt as trust evaporates.

Alternatives are the key. If one of your approaches doesn't work, be ready to try five more. Do this while keeping sight of your final goals and objectives. Give yourself room to negotiate. If you don't, you're bound to find yourself in one or more of the following traps:

❑ Loss of potential options to settle.

❑ Failure to achieve goals.

❑ Appearance of unreasonableness.

❑ Creation of ill will.

❑ Damage to a long-term relationship.

Apply this basic negotiation concept, and you will be able to bring most negotiations to a successful close. It is much easier to build room into your positions before you start negotiating than it is to try to maneuver for more room after the negotiations have started. Do yourself a favor and give yourself as much room as possible.

THE FIFTH STEP: DON'T GIVE AWAY TOO MUCH TOO SOON

Nine times out of ten, the businessperson who gives up too much too soon is the one who falls short of his or her goals. To assure balance in a final agreement, concessions need to be well-timed and given away in small portions.

Concessions are your key points of leverage. Don't be too hasty to remove what little leverage you may have with the other party. You may be surprised to learn that, after you have played your final card, your counterpart still has a full deck.

If you are preparing for a long, cold winter, you wouldn't burn your entire supply of wood on the first cold day. Instead, you would burn each piece as if it were your last, consuming it only when you felt it was absolutely necessary to do so.

Never give up a position without getting something in return. Every concession you offer has value, however small. Understand and define that value. Modern negotiation is not a process where one side makes all the demands, and the other side makes all the concessions. It is a two-way street. Concessions should be exchanged with your counterparts, not extracted from them.

One other problem often arises in giving up too much too soon. The other party may be left with the perception of not getting a good deal—even if he did. It's natural for us to feel that the things we don't have to struggle for are hardly worth having.

There is a definite advantage to be gained by handing out your concessions one by one. Aside from helping you to stay better organized in your negotiations, your opponents will appreciate your concessions more if they have to work harder to get them.

By giving up too much too soon, you virtually guarantee the following problems:

❑ Loss of leverage with your counterpart.

❑ Dissatisfaction with the final agreement.

❑ Inability to gain further concessions from the other party.

❑ Perception that you have given up too much and the other party has not given up enough.

❑ Gain of momentum by your counterpart.

Protect your concessions. They are precious. Don't be too eager to say "yes". Give yourself and the other party time to work through all of the issues before you let go of concessions. Finally, make sure that concessions are exchanged with your partner, not forced from him.

THE SIXTH STEP: BE PREPARED TO SAY NO

The word "no" is the secret weapon in the arsenal of every professional negotiator. It is also one of the most difficult words to use in a negotiation, even for professional negotiators. When the going gets tough, however, the tough just say "no!"

If your employee asks for a week off, but his support is essential for completion of a major project due during that week, you have to be prepared to say "no"—regardless of your concern for the feelings of the employee.

If your boss has given you an assignment with a truly impossible deadline, you have to be prepared to say "no," and work out a schedule that makes more sense.

The next time a government bureaucrat wants you to answer 10 pages of irrelevant questions before he will process your application, be prepared to say "no"!

For this technique to be effective, you have to really believe in what you are saying, and then be able to back up your response with hard facts and rationale. The simple act of saying "no" is not enough by itself. Without a logical rationale, the other party will think that you are being unreasonable and will respond in kind.

It all comes down to the nature of your beliefs. Do you really believe in what you are saying?

Have you ever tried to defend a position that you did not believe in? I can tell you from personal experience that it is almost impossible. It's the same as trying to sell an idea or product that you don't believe in. If you don't believe what you are saying, the other party can read it in your voice and on your face. Don't think that you are fooling anybody! If you don't really believe in what you are saying, you can be sure that the other party will sense it as soon as you try to defend your artificial position.

The word "no" is probably the most powerful word in the English language. Learn how to harness its power,

and you will be able to control the majority of your negotiations. Fail to recognize and apply its power, and you
will be hard-pressed to achieve your goals.

THE SEVENTH STEP: MAKE YOUR WORD YOUR BOND

The most serious sin we can commit as businesspeople is
to renege on an agreement. There is absolutely nothing
worse than concluding an agreement only to have the
other party back out of it.

Sometimes we make honest mistakes. If the mistake is
so grievous that we can't live with it, then, by all means,
retract it. This should, however, be done only in the most
serious circumstance; it must not be taken lightly. If you
develop a reputation for changing your mind after a deal
has been finalized, then how can *anyone* trust anything
you say? Why should they, after all? If you don't back up
your words with action, people will have no basis to trust
a word you say.

If you have made a mistake in a negotiation, your first
priority is to assess the seriousness of the mistake. If the
mistake is not too serious, you should make every effort
not to disturb the final agreement. It is infinitely better to
maintain goodwill with your counterpart by living with
your mistake than to confront him or her with a request
to overturn or amend the agreement.

If you do make a mistake and decide to honor it, be sure
to let your counterpart know about it. You should get as
much goodwill as you can out of the fact that you have
made an error but are willing to live by your commitment
and leave the settlement undisturbed. While you might be

embarrassed or otherwise reticent to admit your error, this simple act can gain you miles of credibility in a long-term relationship. This credibility may be very valuable to you if your counterpart is ever in the same situation and decides to return the favor.

Credibility is something that takes time to develop. Once developed, however, you've got to guard your credibility at any cost. The simplest, and usually the least expensive, thing you can do to gain and protect credibility is to honor your commitments. Stick by your agreements, even if it sometimes hurts; 99 percent of the time it's the best thing to do.

WORKSHEETS

Now that you have learned about the seven basic steps in conducting a business negotiation, it's time to put theory into practice. The following checklist provides a concise and easily applied outline of the different elements involved in conducting a successful negotiation. While it is not absolutely necessary that you complete each and every step before you start a negotiation, the more steps you *do* complete, the greater your probability of success.

The First Step: Be Prepared

Nothing is more important to the ultimate success of your negotiation than preparation. If you do nothing else, at least take the time to complete the following steps before you start.

❑ Familiarize yourself with the background and history of the situation.

❑ Research the issues and topics thoroughly.

❑ Anticipate your counterpart's tactics.

❑ Anticipate your counterpart's rationale.

❑ Develop your positions.

❑ Develop rationale for your positions.

The Second Step: Maximize Your Alternatives

Win-win negotiating requires that you maximize your options and alternatives so that you will be able to identify and agree to mutually satisfactory outcomes with your counterpart.

❑ List your basic goals.

❑ List every possible alternative approach to attaining your goals.

❑ List your key approaches to attaining your goals.

❑ List your counterpart's goals.

❑ List every possible alternative approach to attaining their goals.

❑ List their anticipated approaches to attaining their goals.

The Third Step: Negotiate with the Right Person

If you're not negotiating with the right person, you are probably wasting your time. The following checklist will help you test the limits of your counterpart's authority.

❑ Identify the kinds of decisions your counterpart can make.

❑ Determine the boundaries of those decisions.

❑ Match your situation to your counterpart's authority.

❑ Determine who else in the organization might have to approve the decision.

❑ Quantify how long it will take to secure approvals.

The Fourth Step: Give Yourself Room to Maneuver

Flexibility is a crucial negotiation attribute. Use the following checklist to ensure that you have the tools available to maintain flexibility in your approaches and positions.

❑ Review your basic goals.

❑ Review your counterpart's basic goals.

❑ Determine your minimum acceptable positions.

❑ Determine your counterpart's minimum acceptable positions.

❑ List your common interests.

❑ Review your lists of alternative approaches.

❑ List the goals you are willing to compromise to reach your basic goals.

The Fifth Step: Don't Give Away Too Much Too Soon

Giving away too much too soon is a common and fatal error for many negotiators—especially those who are not comfortable with the negotiation process.

- ❏ List all of your possible concessions.
- ❏ Rank order your concessions.
- ❏ Determine what you will expect in exchange for your concessions.

The Sixth Step: Be Prepared to Say No

"No" is probably the most powerful word in the English language. To be able to defend your goals, you have to learn to use the word no. It's not enough to just say no, however. By working through the following steps, you will be able to justify your requests.

- ❏ Review your basic goals.
- ❏ Review your minimum acceptable positions.
- ❏ Rationalize your reasons for saying no.
- ❏ Provide acceptable alternatives.

The Seventh Step: Make Your Word Your Bond

Do everything you can to follow through on your promises. In a long-term business relationship, credibility is one of your most valuable assets.

- ❏ List your commitments.
- ❏ Determine the actions necessary to follow through on your commitments.
- ❏ Ensure that you have the authority to enforce your commitments.
- ❏ Elicit the support of your co-workers.

Chapter Three

Beware: A Guide to Negotiation Tactics

With all great deceivers there is a noteworthy occurrence to which they owe their power. In the actual act of deception they are overcome by belief in themselves: it is this which then speaks so miraculously and compellingly to those who surround them.

Friedrich Wilhelm Nietzsche

If you can gain a basic command of the most common tactics that you are likely to encounter in the normal course of doing business, you will be able to effectively counter them when they are used against you.

Most of these tactics are holdovers from the old style of win-lose negotiation. The tactics all have one thing in common: to be effective, they rely on some form of pressure directed by one party against another. Whether that pressure derives from position, power, knowledge, time, or coercion, the basic motivation driving the application of these techniques does not promote a cooperative and reasoned approach to negotiation.

Just because the old-style, win-lose tactics are not currently in vogue, however, does not mean that they have gone away. Quite the contrary. These techniques are still widely utilized by many businesspeople, not necessarily because the party using the tactic is trying to take advantage of his counterpart (although that is the net result), but often merely because these are the only techniques he has been taught. Perhaps you have used them yourself from time to time.

I WANT IT ALL

What's the old saying? Buy low, sell high? Some negotiators would argue that you should give as little as possible, and take as much as you can get. While I do not personally subscribe to this philosophy, you will certainly encounter it in your business dealings.

You've got to learn to identify this tactic when it is used against you, and be prepared to counter it. Let's see how this tactic might be used in a typical business negotiation.

My company leased space in a large office building. With the original five-year lease about to expire, we were considering two options: either renewing our lease if we could get a decrease in our rent, or finding new, less-expensive alternatives.

* * * * *

"Let me begin, Steve, by saying that we are very pleased to have your company as a tenant in this building. In the five years that you have rented space from us, we have developed a good relationship. I have brought copies of the proposed lease agreement with me. I don't see why we shouldn't be able to get through this quickly and have everything wrapped by this afternoon."

"Thank you, Carol. We also value the relationship that we have developed with you over the years. We hope to preserve that relationship in the next lease term. If the terms and conditions in the proposed lease are to everyone's satisfaction, I'm very confident we'll be able to wrap this up with a minimum of difficulty."

"Please turn to page three of the agreement, Steve. I have summarized the main points in Table 1. Let's go through them one by one. To begin, we are proposing a nominal increase of five percent over your current rate for the first three years of the agreement. Then, in years four and five, there would be additional increases of five and six percent, respectively. We feel that this is quite reasonable considering the unpredictability of the current economic situation. While this may be a little above the Consumer Price Index, we feel that this is a reasonable number."

"Five percent! Are you serious, Carol?"

"Yes, Steve, we're quite serious about this proposal. The CPI was approximately 4.5 percent last year. Five percent is right in the ballpark."

"That may be true, Carol, but you know that vacancy rates are at an all-time high. This whole area is overbuilt. From what I've read in the papers, some of the landlords are getting so desperate that they're offering a year's free rent if you'll commit to a five-year lease. I'll bet if I shopped around a little bit, I could find a much better deal."

"I can't deny that the market is getting ugly, but we have a list of potential tenants who would love to pick up your space. One more thing, have you considered what it would cost to move? You might save a few pennies elsewhere, but you'll pay a lot more in the long run if you have to move your entire operation."

"Yeah, I know, Carol. It would be a real pain to have to move."

"Steve, we want to keep you as a tenant. We would be willing to go with a four percent increase over the current rate for years one through three if you'll go with our proposed increases of five and six percent for years four and five. What do you think?"

* * * * *

The above negotiation shows the classic technique of starting high, then giving away a small concession to try to elicit a higher-value concession in return from the other party. It is anyone's guess as to whether the parties will finally resolve their differences and reach an agreement which is in the mutual interest of both parties. By giving away a little, and taking a lot, one party is using pressure to push the agreement.

Typically, this results in a clear win-lose situation. If the participants don't achieve at least some of their goals, you can be sure that any agreement will be one-sided and inherently unstable. In addition, development of a long-term relationship may be jeopardized when the losing party realizes that he or she has been victimized.

The most effective way to counter this technique, if it is used against you, is to have a very clear understanding of your goals and objectives. The party applying the "give a little" tactic hopes that, for each concession, you will feel obliged to follow with a concession of your own—hopefully one that has much higher value. Know when to walk away from a negotiation. If you are doing all the giving and your own interests are not being addressed and satisfied, it is time to find alternatives to meet your needs.

GOOD COP, BAD COP

You've seen those old reruns of *Dragnet, Kojak,* and *Cagney and Lacey* a million times. You know, the ones where a suspect is being interrogated alternately by a big, mean police investigator who plays the role of "bad cop," and then by his syrupy-sweet partner who plays the role of "good cop."

The first interrogator is invariably the bad cop. He's the guy who shines a bright light in the prisoner's face and refuses to let him go to the bathroom until he confesses. During this phase, the bad cop is verbally abusive as he conducts a methodical psychological hazing. Threats are made with the sole aim of breaking down the will of the prisoner. Eventually, just as the prisoner really begins to sweat, the bad cop will leave. In comes the good cop. He has a completely different attitude.

The good cop will immediately become the prisoner's best friend. The good cop will remove the restraints, let the suspect have some freedom to move around, and be openly sympathetic to his plight. The prisoner is often so happy to have found someone he can trust that he will spill the beans and confess his crime.

While most business situations are not quite as dramatic, the very same technique is often applied during the negotiation process. The standard scenario goes like this:

During the presentation of the opposing party's proposal, one member of the team suddenly slams the table and insists that the terms and conditions being offered are completely unreasonable. He becomes completely unglued, and rants and raves about every aspect of the proposal. As far as he is concerned, there's no way he would sign an agreement like this.

After the team member has stomped out of the meeting to further make his point, a teammate, playing the role of the good cop, will be very sympathetic to the opposition and say, "I still believe we can come to an agreement. Let's see if we can't compromise and wrap this up."

If this technique has been as effective as planned, the opponent will be softened up by the explosion of the bad cop and drawn into an agreement—one that will likely not be in his favor—by the good cop.

In my county, there has been a long-standing battle between those who wish to develop new commercial and residential projects, and those who favor protecting what little undeveloped space remains as a legacy to future generations. Those who support development cite the potential economic benefits to the area through job creation and increased business opportunities. Those who oppose property development warn of the potential for destruction of sensitive ecological habitats and the certain degradation of the quality of life for current residents.

One such example was the effort by a large, politically well-connected builder to develop a parcel in an ecologically-sensitive zone within the urbanizing area. To proceed with this development, the builder had to seek the approval of the County Planning Commission.

* * * * *

"Good afternoon. My name is Kingsley Thomas, and I represent Kruger Homes. I'm here today to discuss the development of a mixed residential/commercial project."

"Yes, Ms. Thomas, we've been expecting you. I'm Tom Dickenson. This is my planning aide, Sue Hoskins."

"Pleased to meet both of you."

"Let's get right down to business, Ms. Thomas. Tell us about your proposal."

"What we are proposing is the construction of a 1,500-unit, low-density, mixed-use development in the Las Ballenas lagoon site."

"Ms. Thomas, before you go any further, I've got to tell you that Las Ballenas lagoon is a very ecologically-sensitive area. I am dead set against any project at that site. We simply can't afford to allow destruction of this habitat."

"But, Mr. Dickenson, you haven't even heard our proposal yet. If you will give me a few minutes to explain it, I think you'll find that we have satisfied most of the ecological concerns that have been voiced by the local conservationists of this county. It's no secret that the recession still has a grip on the local economy. Approval of this project will guarantee the creation of at least 50 more jobs in the county. That's 50 new taxpayers who are currently drawing unemployment."

"Frankly, Ms. Thomas, I don't give a hoot about jobs in this county. *My* job is to protect the Public Trust. I have watched your company, and others like it, systematically level and scrape almost every piece of undeveloped dirt in this county. Now you want my approval to pave over the last sliver of un-soiled land?"

"But, Mr. Dickenson, members of the Las Ballenas Conservancy have already reviewed our proposal and they have voiced no objections. I can't tell you how important this project will be to the taxpayers of the county. With 1,500 new housing units, plus at least 25 new businesses, that means a substantial increase in the county tax base."

"I don't want to hear any more about this proposal! I'm sick and tired of it!"

Dickenson gets up to leave.

"Sue, I'm going to go back to my office to get some real work done. I've wasted enough time on this ludicrous proposal. You may continue with Ms. Thomas if you like. As far as I'm concerned, I don't want to hear the name Kruger Homes ever again!"

After Dickenson leaves the room, Sue Hoskins opens the conversation.

"Kingsley, I'm sorry about my boss's behavior. I hope that he didn't upset you."

"No, Sue, I'm fine. He's just so unreasonable! I can't understand why he won't listen to our proposal."

"I know what you mean, Kingsley. I find him hard to deal with myself sometimes. But maybe there *is* a way that we can get him to consider your proposal."

"Do you really think so, Sue?"

"Sure, I think I can make some progress with him. Let's start by cutting your proposed units from 1,500 to 500. . . ."

* * * * *

Dickenson and Hoskins have astutely played the classic good cop, bad cop ploy. Dickenson was absolutely incorrigible. He attacked Thomas. He attacked Kruger Homes. And he attacked the proposal. In fact, he didn't have a positive thing to say about anything.

After Dickenson stomped out of the room, his assistant, Sue Hoskins, played the trump card in the good cop, bad cop hand. She sympathized with Thomas while advancing a much lower offer for negotiation. Instead of the 1,500 units that Thomas proposed, Hoskins suggested a far lower quantity, 500 units. At this point, it is likely that Thomas will be very happy to get any units approved, much less the 1,500 she originally proposed.

TEAM TACTICS

Another common technique—one that is closely related to the good cop, bad cop technique—is the team tactic. Here, you won't have just one opponent to contend with, but an entire team of negotiators. In its ultimate incarnation, each member of the team possesses specialized expertise in a particular facet of the overall negotiation. One team member is designated as the leader. Depending on the topic, each team member is called upon to argue the team position from his or her unique perspective.

A negotiating team might include, for example, an accountant, a labor specialist, a materials manager, and the company vice president for marketing. Team members will be called upon as necessary to present all the different rationales specific to their particular specialties in support of the overall proposal. The team tactic is most effective when only one or two people stand in opposition to the team. A team negotiation often becomes a rapid-fire presentation of issues and demands that can soon overwhelm a single negotiating party.

Hiring new staff to support an expanding operation is a task that I have had to face many times over the course of my career. In the next example, Pat has decided that, in order to keep up with the increasing workload in his department, he really needs to hire three more employees. He is going to make his request in today's weekly staff meeting. Also attending the meeting are Pat's boss, Debbie; the chief executive officer of the corporation, Luis; the facility manager, Peter; and Liza, the human resources manager. Pat begins the discussion.

* * * * *

"I've recently come to the conclusion that I'm going to need to recruit three new employees over the next few months."

Luis is the first to speak up:

"Three new employees? You know the company can't afford that now. Aren't you aware that we just took a big hit to our year-end reserves?"

"No, I wasn't aware of that, Luis. But that doesn't change the staffing issue in my department. I need some help."

Liza joins in:

"Pat, I don't see how you could need any more help. Didn't we just recruit four new hires for you last fiscal year? I thought you told me back then that you would be set for the next couple of years. Why do you need more people already?"

"When I submitted my original request, I didn't anticipate the growth in my department's responsibilities. It has now become apparent that we can't keep up with the increased workload."

Peter, the facilities manager, steps in:

"Pat, even if we did hire the three people, where would you put them? We simply don't have the space, much less the computers, furniture, or anything else. If we hire more people, we'll have to lease additional space someplace. That will cost us."

Pat's boss, Debbie, speaks up:

"You know, Pat, I have to agree with what everyone else is saying. I don't think we can afford to hire three people, much less find a place for them to work in our current building. Rethink your situation and see if you can't get more out of the resources you already have."

* * * * *

When you are confronted with team tactics, unless you are uncommonly well prepared, it's hard to not be overwhelmed by all the facts and figures at the team's fingertips. There are two ways to effectively counter the use of this tactic.

The first approach is to fight fire with fire and form a team of your own. Just as the opposing team had representatives from all specialties, so can your team. Each of your team members can be specifically selected and assigned to refute their counterparts on the other team.

The second possible approach is for you to face the team alone, but to be well prepared in all aspects of the negotiation. Take a very deliberate and methodical approach, and refuse to be stampeded by the team. If you are firm, and stand your ground, you will be able to effectively counter the use of team tactics against you.

APPROVAL APPROACH

Everyone you deal with in a business situation has some limitations on their authority or power. Aides are limited by supervisors. Supervisors are limited by managers. Managers are limited by vice presidents. Vice presidents are limited by presidents.

Approval authority, or the lack thereof, can be a very effective tool in the negotiation process. You have undoubtedly been involved in many situations where the person you are trying to persuade says that he doesn't have the authority. Instead, he says that he will have to get his boss's approval first.

I will have to be honest and admit that I have used this technique to achieve my goals in the past. I have since found that it is better to be up-front with your limitations. This will make the negotiation a cooperative effort in which you and your counterpart seek ways to achieve your mutual goals, instead of a one-sided victory achieved through trickery.

In one case, I was negotiating a deal for some new computers. Carefully note how I used approval tactics to extract concessions from Tony, the sales representative.

* * * * *

"All right, Peter. We've been through my proposal. What do you think? I have the contracts all ready to sign."

"Tony, I think you should know something. The agreement that you have proposed is above my limit of authority. I'm not authorized to approve any action above $25,000. Any purchase above that amount has to be approved by our board. Since the computers you have offered cost $27,500, I don't have the authority to sign."

"That's quite a surprise, Peter. I thought you said you had the authority to commit the company for all purchases. You want to get this equipment in place as soon as possible, right? How long is it going to take for you to get approval from the board?"

"It could be months. Tony, we really do want those computers. We're all looking forward to the day when we can get rid of those old PCs. We'll be very disappointed if we can't get them in here as soon as possible. I guess the only other alternative would be if you could drop the price of the computers under $25,000. Then I could sign the contracts right now. Do you think that might be possible?"

* * * * *

Do you think Tony dropped his price? You bet he did. I played my trump card perfectly. I used an authority limitation to give Tony little choice. He had two options. He could hold his price at $27,500 and risk losing the sale, or he could drop the price under $25,000 and be assured of the sale. Of course, many other factors may work into his decision to drop the price.

How many times have you personally settled for something less than you wanted because the person you were dealing with had limited authority? We have all been on the receiving end of this tactic.

The best defense against the use of approval tactics is to be patient. Often, the party who uses the tactic is testing you to see if you are willing to make a concession. If you don't immediately cave in, you may find to your surprise that your counterpart is willing to conclude the agreement in very short order. Even if the agreement really does have to be approved at a higher level, patience is the best way to avoid being taken advantage of through the use of approval tactics.

Don't assume, however, that when someone says he has limited authority that this is necessarily the case. This tactic is very popular with people who really *do* have the authority they pretend not to have. If you call their bluff, you may find that authority, or the lack thereof, was not the issue after all.

TIME WARP

Using time as a weapon is another classic negotiation technique. Time tactics can be used in many different ways. Discussion of the most common time tactics will help you develop techniques to defend yourself when they are used against you.

One method of using time as a negotiation tactic is to limit it. Salespeople, in particular, love to use this tactic. Time limitations can also be used quite effectively in business to force a decision.

The key to the use of this tactic is to limit the amount of time that an offer is put forward for consideration. At the end of this finite period, the offer is withdrawn. Of course, the other party is notified at the outset that the offer on the table is only good for a set period of time. For this tactic to work effectively, the user has to communicate the time limitation to the other party. With no time limitation, no motivation will be gained.

Just the other day, a sales representative attempted to use a time limitation to get me to agree to a contract for mail sorting services.

The company, let's call it Mail-Fast, had been trying to line us up as a customer for six months. Jackie, the Mail-Fast sales representative, was persistent. Although we kept putting her off, she kept trying to sell the benefits of her company's services.

*   *   *   *   *

"So, Peter, have you had a chance to review the brochure I sent you?"

"As a matter of fact, I have, Jackie. I'm still not clear about what your service will do for us. Why don't you explain it to me."

"Sure, I would be happy to. You know that the Postal Service offers all sorts of different discounts on postage for customers who are willing to presort their mail or use nine-digit zip codes."

"Yes, I'm generally familiar with the programs."

"Okay. What we offer is a service that is guaranteed to save you money on your postage. All you need to do is address and seal your envelopes as you normally do. There's no need for you to use the full nine-digit zip—just use the five-digit number. Our computers will do the rest. Then, run the envelopes through your postage meter at the bulk rate and toss them in our bin for pickup. We'll schedule your facility for a 4 P.M. time slot."

"I'm not sure I understand the advantage of contracting the mail sorting out to Mail-Fast."

"That's what I'm getting to, Peter. Once we receive the mail, our computer equipment automatically reads the addresses and sprays a bar code on each envelope corresponding to the full nine-digit zip code. The machines then sort the mail for delivery to the main Post Office so that the bulk presort rate applies to your mail. You will save by not having a person devoted to sorting mail for the Post Office. You will also save directly through the lower postage rate."

"Okay, I understand now."

"There's one thing you need to know, Peter. We've been holding the 4 P.M. slot open for you for several months. We can only keep it available for your organization through next Friday. If you aren't ready to sign up by then, we'll have to give the slot to someone else."

* * * * *

The use of time limitation tactics can be a very effective way to get someone to make a decision. The best way to ensure that you are not taken advantage of through their use is to be prepared to call your counterpart's bluff. While some time limits are real, many are not. You'll often find that, if you test your counterpart, what seemed real was not.

Another technique for using time warp is the exact opposite of the way it was used in the above example. Instead of using deadlines to apply pressure, the negotiator uses delays. Stalling, ignoring, and delaying are all manifestations of this ploy.

This technique is best applied when a party is in a position of tactical advantage. While deadlines create pressure to make a quick decision, delays create pressure to land the big fish before it jumps off the hook. Either way, both techniques tend to throw the recipient off balance.

Due to the resignation of the marketing coordinator, our company's proposal efforts were in serious jeopardy. The corporation pulled out all the stops to find a new marketing coordinator as soon as possible.

After weeks of searching, the company finally found the right candidate. Winifred possessed just the right combination of training and hands-on experience. However, at the time, she was working happily for a competitor. Let's see how the story unfolded.

* * * * *

"I'm glad you agreed to discuss the position with us, Winifred. We've been looking high and low for a new marketing coordinator and you're the person for the job."

"Thanks for your confidence. As I mentioned when we spoke on the phone, I do enjoy my current job, but I am certainly willing to hear what you have to say."

"We understand. We don't want to do anything to jeopardize your current position. However, we do have quite an opportunity here for the right person."

"Let's hear it."

"As marketing coordinator for our company, you would be in charge of the entire proposal effort. You would also have your own staff and your own budget. We're scheduled to submit seven different proposals over the next eight weeks. We would expect you to take charge right away."

"So far, so good. How much does this position pay?"

"We thought you would ask that question. At this time, we are prepared to offer $35,000 per year. This, of course, is in addition to our generous benefits package."

"Let me think about this. I'll get back to you as soon as I've decided."

"That sounds fine, Winifred. We hope that you'll favorably consider our offer. The upcoming proposal efforts need to be kicked-off very soon. We hope that you'll get back to us right away."

"I promise that I will give it my immediate attention."

A few days passed, and we still had not heard back from Winifred. Management was concerned that, if the marketing coordinator was not hired soon, the proposals would be in trouble. It was decided that a call should be made to Winifred to see if she had made her decision yet.

"Winifred?"

"Yes?"

"This is Tom Marks, director of human resources here at . . ."

"Oh, hello, Tom. I bet you're calling about the marketing coordinator position."

"That's right. We were hoping that we would hear from you by now. Have you made a decision yet regarding our job offer?"

"No. I've been thinking about it, but I haven't decided yet. To be frank with you, I was more than a little disappointed with the salary offer. For the caliber of person needed to get the job done, $35,000 is not adequate. I'm thinking more in terms of $40,000."

"Geez, Winifred. I don't know if we'll be able to swing that. Since you didn't raise any objections during our meeting a few days ago, we thought that you were satisfied with the contents of the offer. This is a real shocker. We had not considered any alternatives to our offer. We're banking on your starting with the company in time to kick off the upcoming proposal effort. You're going to be critical to our success . . . we need you to start right away."

"I like it where I am. I suppose I could stay a few more years, if necessary. I'm not in any big rush to move."

"I will have to go back to management and talk to them about this. We feel that the offer that we made to you is quite fair."

"If you can increase the offer, I'll be glad to talk further with you about this position. I am very confident that I would be able to quickly take charge of your proposals. I'm looking forward to hearing any changes that you would be willing to make to your offer."

* * * * *

Winifred has used delaying tactics to create time pressure on the other party. By simply delaying a final decision, she has created an environment more favorable to the achievement of her goals. She knows full well that the company is increasingly desperate to sign her. Winifred holds all the cards and she can call the shots.

For this technique to work optimally, the person using it has to have leverage. Therein lies the key to defending yourself against the use of delaying tactics. If your counterpart doesn't have real leverage, or, at least, the appearance of real leverage, she won't be able to effectively use this tactic against you. If, for example, Winifred had just been fired when she was approached by the recruiter, she might feel more vulnerable. This would make it more difficult for Winifred to maintain her leverage over the other party. Rather than take the chance that she might lose this opportunity, Winifred might be tempted to accept the first offer.

If you can remove the source of leverage, you can defuse the power of delaying tactics. Question your counterpart. Find out if there are any hidden motivations. Generally, the easiest way to counter delaying tactics is to have as many alternatives and options at your disposal as possible. When your counterpart finally realizes that she doesn't have leverage, she will be much more willing to negotiate with you in a cooperative, win-win manner.

POWER PLAYS

Power plays describe a wide variety of situations in which one party achieves his goals merely by the exertion of his power over the other negotiating party. You probably see this technique used most frequently by people in your organization who are authoritarian in manner. Even people who are not normally authoritarian may use this tactic from time to time—if only as a not-so-subtle reminder to the other party that they are to be respected.

Power tactics are not dissimilar to the way that animals in the wild establish their dominance over other animals in their communities. Wolves in a pack establish their dominance by fighting with other wolves. Once an animal has risen to the top of the hierarchy, he no longer has to fight to maintain his status. Instead, mere gestures or threats of violence will maintain the status quo. Threat gestures are used in much the same way as power plays are used in a negotiation.

A very common example, one that I faced almost daily in my former role as director of administration for a research and development firm, is the request by program managers for reports that show some specific aspect of financial or project accounting data. In our business, it was very important that all non-administrative personnel charge their time directly to customer-funded projects or contracts. If a non-administrative employee was not directly charging a project, that meant he was charging overhead instead. If this practice were allowed to continue uncontrolled, we would price ourselves right out of the market.

The group manager, Terry, asked my controller, Sydney, to develop a weekly report showing the percentage of time charged directly to customers for each of the 100+ employees in our group. The report was intended to highlight employees who were charging too much of their time to overhead.

* * * * *

"What we need, Sydney, is a report that shows, on an employee-by-employee basis, the percentage of their time charged to direct projects each week. I've got to have this report immediately. Are you going to have any problems supporting this request?"

"As a matter of fact, yes, I do have a problem supporting your request. We're currently preparing to migrate our management information system onto a new computer, and we're up to our ears in work right now. We can probably get to your request in a couple of weeks."

"Sydney, this shouldn't be a big deal. I'm sure the data is readily available. All I'm asking for is a weekly report of percent direct. I can't imagine that it would take more than an hour or two for someone on your staff to write a routine to generate the report every week."

"That may be true, Terry, but I just can't spare anybody's time right now. I'm sorry, but that's just the way it is."

"This report was a personal request from the president. I guess I'll have to let him know that you're not going to be able to support his request. I was hoping we would be able to work this out."

"Wait a minute, Terry. Let's see if I can't find someone to put on this project right away. I'll let you know when we're done."

* * * * *

When you want to get something done, a little power goes a long way. Terry used the authority of the president of the company to exert power over the group controller. This way, Terry will achieve the goal of getting the monthly report established. Sydney decided it's probably not in his interest to fight this particular issue. Of course, Sydney and Terry could easily have reversed their roles. Next time it could be Sydney who has a request to make of Terry. In that particular situation, it may be Sydney who has the power to get his project accomplished.

That's the way power is. Power can be transitory and, during the course of a negotiation, it can shift back and forth between parties many times. You may feel that you need a scorecard to keep track of who has the power at any given time.

Power is one of the easiest and most effective tools used in business negotiations. It is therefore one of the most commonly applied business negotiation tactics. Countering its use against you can be a very difficult proposition.

In business, power tactics are most often applied by someone who wants a request to receive immediate attention, or to be the highest priority. The most effective counter, therefore, is to fully understand your own priorities, and the relative priority of your counterpart's requests. You may have real limitations that prevent you from immediately granting every request you receive. Your counterpart may also have very real priorities that require immediate attention.

With that basic information in hand, you can then co-operatively work out solutions that address your mutual needs. Instead of being merely knee-jerk reactions to the egotistical use of power plays, your solutions will instead be grounded in reasoned assessments that hold the needs of the business as the first and foremost priority.

MONEY CRUNCH

Money crunch describes the situation in which one party uses money as a negotiating tool. A party applying the money-crunch technique will say that he cannot meet a particular request due to financial constraints. He will claim he is limited to a certain amount of money for a particular reason, and then go on to rationalize that reason.

Money constraints can come from many different sources. The person using a money-crunch tactic may say that his budget does not allow for any additional expenditures, or that his funds are already committed to other projects.

The use of money-crunch techniques is very common in business, particularly in the acquisition of goods and services. The following example clearly illustrates the kind of money-crunch situation that I commonly encountered when I closed deals with my customers for contracted computer support services.

* * * * *

"Thanks for flying out to see us today, Peter. We're pleased that you consider us an important enough customer to go through the expense and trouble of this personal visit."

"It's my pleasure. We have always considered you to be one of our most important customers. You may not know it, Kim, but your organization awarded us our first contract."

"No, I didn't know that."

"We have always prided ourselves on the work we do for you. That's why we are especially pleased to be able to offer our support to your new data operation."

"Thank you, Peter. Why don't you tell me exactly what you propose to do for us?"

"I have personally analyzed your equipment setup, and the quantity of data that you expect to input on a daily basis, to arrive at an optimum staffing profile based on your projections. This staff, which would consist of a supervisor, a programmer/ analyst, and five key entry operators, will be able to meet your needs well into the future."

"That sounds fine, Peter. I realize that the work fluctuates from day to day depending on where we are in our accounting cycle. Tell me, will your proposed staff be able to handle the big crunches when we run payroll and month-end reports?"

"Sure, that's not going to be a problem. We'll just run a double shift to take care of the extra workload."

"Super. So what's the bottom line?"

"$175,000."

"Hmmm . . . I'm sure that your price is a fair one, but it looks like we're going to have a problem."

"What problem might that be?"

"The problem is that my budget is $150,000 for this service. That's my bottom line. There's no way I'll be able to get an increase. I'm lucky to still have that much, considering the equipment overruns in the rest of my budget for the new data operation."

"You're sure about that, Kim?"

"Unfortunately, yes. Is there some way you can reduce your price and still get all of our work done on time?"

"I'm sure there has to be some way we can swing it. Let me go back to the drawing board and come up with some options. I'm going to run to my hotel right now. I'll be back here by 3 P.M."

* * * * *

Of course, I didn't know whether or not Kim truly was constrained by the amount of money that she had available. I had little choice, however, but to rely upon her statements and then try to work within her limits. In the above example, Kim's data operation support budget for the year might have actually been $200,000. I had no way of finding out whether that was the case or not. As far as I was concerned, I could either choose to work within the stated limits, or forget the deal.

The easiest, and the riskiest, way to tell if someone is using money-crunch ploys against you is to call his bluff. Communicate your offer, be firm, and stand by it. If necessary, just walk away. If the other party was bluffing, it's likely that you will know right away. The opponent who utilized a money ploy will be back soon with a more favorable offer in hand. When this happens, you'll know that you have a high probability of achieving your goals.

If the other party doesn't come back with a new offer after you call his bluff, then it's very possible that the money constraint is real. You'll then have to decide whether you are willing to modify your own goals to achieve an agreement that meets both of your needs.

ULTIMATUMS

No one likes ultimatums—except, perhaps, those who deliver them. There is something about ultimatums that make their use patently objectionable to most business-people. We all want to have options and alternatives in our business dealings, and we don't like to be dictated to. It is therefore very important to be able to deal with ultimatums in a rational way, and not let our emotions get the best of us.

In negotiation, most ultimatums present themselves as take-it-or-leave-it offers. Instead of allowing for flexibility or alternatives, one party presents an offer with only two possible responses: either accept the offer exactly as it has been presented or forget the deal.

If both sides are not willing to make at least minor concessions during the course of a negotiation, someone will end up the loser in the deal. Aside from the creation of ill will, the loser will not be fully committed to the agreement that is finally reached.

If you are given a ultimatum, you must be prepared to act decisively and immediately. Ask yourself the following questions:

❑ Can you still achieve the goals that you seek within the constraints of the ultimatum?

❑ Do you think that the other party is bluffing with the use of an ultimatum?

❑ What would happen if you called that bluff by turning the other party down?

❑ Can you walk away from the offer?

❑ Can you reasonably expect your counterpart to enter into a negotiation that considers the goals and interests that you both share?

People who use ultimatums generally feel that they have some form of leverage over their opponents. To counter an ultimatum, determine if the party really has any leverage in that particular situation, and what the basis of that leverage is. To overturn an ultimatum, you must negate that leverage. As was the case with delaying tactics, the best solution is to have alternatives and options available. Ultimatums only work when the target has no other options.

Understand that ultimatum demands are often made from a position of perceived power, and not real power. Before accepting any ultimatum, make an effort to determine the full extent of the options available to you. At a minimum, be prepared to call your counterpart's bluff and to reject the proposal, if necessary.

If the other party was indeed bluffing, you will quickly find out after you have rejected his demands. He will then come back with a counter proposal that backs off of the original ultimatum position. You can then continue with the negotiation in the newly found spirit of mutual cooperation.

If the ultimatum is real and, after you have called his bluff, he still refuses to budge, you can then determine whether or not the agreement is really of importance to you. If it is, you may want to accede to his requests. If you decide you do not want to accept his demands, then by all means reject the offer.

You may not want to accept an offer as a matter of principle. Regardless of the fact that it may be in your immediate interest to accept the ultimatum, you may not want to set such a precedent. If you continue to back up these words with deeds, the other party will eventually get the point that you cannot be railroaded. Once you make it clear that you won't be a victim, the other party will be left with no other choice but to discontinue the use of ultimatums.

In any case, don't let ultimatums thwart you from pursuing your own goals. Carefully analyze the ultimatum and determine if it is in your interest to accept or reject it. You may find that, in certain circumstance, it is in your interest to accept an ultimatum. In many cases, however, it is best to stand your ground and refuse to be intimidated through the use of ultimatum techniques.

Make it clear that, if your counterpart wishes to do business with you in the future, it will only be done through a fair give-and-take process, where alternatives are explored cooperatively and solutions are decided on a mutually beneficial basis.

WORKSHEETS

While win-win negotiating has been in vogue for the past several years, many businesspeople still believe in the old-school, win-lose style of negotiating. You have to be prepared, when faced with a win-lose negotiator, to counter his tactics. Use the following checklists to identify the most commonly used win-lose negotiation ploys.

I Want It All

By making an extreme offer, and then granting concessions grudgingly, if at all, the negotiator hopes to wear down your resolve. You will know that you have met such a negotiator when you encounter the following traits:

- ❑ Your counterpart's first offer is extreme.
- ❑ Minor concessions are made grudgingly.
- ❑ You are pressured to make significant concessions.
- ❑ Your counterpart refuses to reciprocate.

Good Cop, Bad Cop

The practitioners of this tactic hope to sway you to their side by alternating sympathetic with threatening behavior. Be on your guard when you are confronted with the following actions:

- ❑ Your counterpart becomes irrational or abusive.
- ❑ One party walks out of a negotiation.
- ❑ Irrational behavior is followed by reasonable, sympathetic behavior.

Team Tactics

Unless you have prepared thoroughly for your negotiation, it is easy to be overwhelmed by the use of team tactics. Team tactics will manifest themselves in the following ways:

- ❑ The other party consists of more than one person.
- ❑ Each member of the opposing team is specialized.
- ❑ You are overwhelmed with a fast-paced presentation.
- ❑ Your counterpart objects to your forming your own team.

Approval Approach

To gain an advantage, negotiators will sometimes pretend to lack authority to approve an agreement. This tactic will generally follow one of the following patterns:

- ❑ The other party has more authority than he or she will admit to.
- ❑ The deal is linked to getting approval from a higher authority.
- ❑ Concessions are requested to coincide with your counterpart's limited authority.
- ❑ If you call his bluff, you find that authority is not really the issue.

Time Warp

Time can be used as a very powerful weapon in the arsenal of the win-lose negotiator. When any of the following techniques are used against you, refuse to be forced into an unfavorable position:

- ❑ The offer is valid only for a limited time.
- ❑ You are pressured to accept arbitrary deadlines.
- ❑ Your counterpart stalls or delays the progress of the negotiation.
- ❑ The other party refuses to return your calls.
- ❑ Your counterpart increases pressure on you to settle quickly.

Power Plays

The use of power, whether real or perceived, is another commonly used negotiation tactic. You'll know that power is being used against you when your counterpart applies the following techniques:

- ❑ Your counterpart's negotiation style is authoritarian in nature.
- ❑ The other party threatens to go over your head.
- ❑ Your counterpart drops names.
- ❑ Your counterpart tries to give his needs a higher priority than yours.

Money Crunch

A money crunch occurs when financial constraints are cited as the reason for your counterpart's position.

- ❑ The other party claims that he is subject to certain budget limitations.
- ❑ Your counterpart pressures you to drop your price to meet his needs.
- ❑ When you call the other party's bluff, the budget limitation disappears.

Ultimatums

Ultimatums are the ultimate negotiation tool for the win-lose negotiator. No other tactic is quite so obviously designed to force a party to submit to the will of the user of this technique. Beware when your counterpart tries any of the following:

- ❑ You are presented with a take-it-or-leave-it offer.
- ❑ The party overtly tries to force you to accept his demands.
- ❑ Your counterpart is unwilling to make concessions.
- ❑ You are expected to make all the concessions.

Chapter Four

The PREP System of Negotiation

Men are not to be judged by what they do not know, but by what they do know, and the manner in which they know it.

Luc de Clapiers Vauvenargues

Preparation is the single most important determinant of a successful negotiation. Every minute or hour spent in preparation will be rewarded many times over when an agreement is finally reached. I have lost count of how many times I have personally witnessed negotiations that have become one-sided, win-lose exercises in futility because one or the other parties was not fully prepared to negotiate.

Have you ever felt that you were being taken advantage of by someone who was in much better command of the facts? Clearly, the party who is best prepared for a negotiation will have a definite advantage over the other party. Has your apparent inexperience ever set off a shark-like feeding frenzy of aggressive negotiating tactics by your counterpart? Unfortunately, the lack of preparation is often a signal to the other party that you are an easy target of opportunity—and potential victim who can be taken advantage of with a minimum of effort.

If you have a full understanding of the other party's background and what he is looking for, and some understanding of where he wants to go with the agreement, you will have a tremendous advantage over anyone who has not researched your background and situations. Only *you* will be able to fully understand the real and perceived needs of your counterpart, and be able to present mutually beneficial alternatives that address those needs.

The PREP system discusses the essential steps involved in preparing for the negotiation process. My goal in presenting it is to provide you with the basic tools to conduct a well researched and effective negotiation. The better prepared you are, the higher the probability that you will be able to present a wide range of alternatives that will ultimately lead to a cooperatively negotiated agreement that is fair and in the best interests of both parties.

PREP

Many everyday business activities involve some element of negotiation. As with most business activities, the better prepared you are for a negotiation, the more successful you can expect to be in reaching your goals. The PREP system provides you with a proven, logical framework to use in preparing for a business negotiation. The acronym PREP stands for:

Preview your goals.

Research the topic.

Evaluate your counterpart.

Prepare your rationale.

The PREP system represents the four major steps that are essential in preparing for a business negotiation. Each step is equally important and, to maximize your effectiveness, should be completed before a negotiation is initiated.

This goes doubly for those times when you are caught off guard. Never allow yourself to be brow-beaten into a negotiation for which you are not prepared. It will rarely be in your interest to do so. Instead, call a time-out, and take all the time you need to prepare for the negotiation by working through these steps:

P: Preview Your Goals

Before you do anything else, identify and prioritize the goals you want to achieve in your negotiation. At the same time, consider all the possible alternatives you can present during the negotiation to help bring the interests of you and your counterpart together.

The thought process you go through to determine your goals and alternatives will help give you direction in the negotiation process. If you don't take the time to determine your goals in advance, it will be that much easier for the other party to short-circuit the collaborative process and impose his goals upon you.

R: Research the Topic

To be fully prepared, it is imperative that you completely and thoroughly research your topic. There is a direct relationship between the amount of time you spend in research and the degree of success that you can expect to achieve in any negotiation. If you do not spend quality time fully researching the issues, you just cannot expect to fully understand the business environment surrounding the negotiation, or to scratch beyond the thinnest layer of possible alternatives.

The more time you devote to research, the better able you will be to convincingly and vigorously present the full range of your goals and alternatives. At the same time, by conducting complete and thorough research in advance of a negotiation, you will have a much better grasp of your counterpart's goals, and be able to collaborate instead of getting trapped into inflexible positions that only serve to create distrust and erode your long-term mutual interests.

E: Evaluate Your Counterpart

Evaluating your counterpart means more than just evaluating the personality or communication style of the person you will be negotiating with. It also means evaluating all the possible assumptions, goals, and alternatives that your counterpart might bring to the negotiation table.

The accurate anticipation of your counterpart's goals and aspirations will help increase your ability to effectively present your own goals and present well thought-out alternatives. Remember, your first priority is to create an agreement that benefits both parties.

Before you begin a negotiation, develop a list of as many potential negotiation scenarios as possible. Then mentally rehearse the different scenarios. This will give you sufficient time to work out possible solutions or alternatives before the negotiation starts.

P: Prepare Your Rationale

The development of a strong rationale for your positions will allow you to defend the goals you identified in the goal-preview phase of the PREP system. Every time you say "no" to an opponent's request, you should have a rationale to justify it.

It is not enough to just say "no." You have to have strong reasons for doing so. Only through this process of rationalization and justification can you expect an opponent to understand your way of thinking. If your counterparts feel that you are rejecting their requests out of hand, you will build walls of resistance and mistrust that will become increasingly difficult to bridge as time goes on. It is, of course, impossible to build a long-term business relationship without a solid foundation of cooperation and trust.

In the sections that follow, you will find further discussion of each component of the PREP system. It is essential that you perform each step before you enter into a negotiation. The complexity of the negotiation will dictate the amount of time you devote to each step. Some negotiations may require days or even weeks of preparation. Others may require only minutes. Whatever the specifics of your situation, the consistent application of each step of the PREP system will ensure your comprehensive and complete preparation for any eventuality.

Don't be intimidated into thinking that the steps involved in this process will take too long. Definitely don't fall into the trap of believing that you already have all the answers. The time involved in preparation, even for highly complex and lengthy negotiations, will be rewarded many times over in the results you achieve. The most important thing, and the overriding reason for applying the PREP system, is to go through the thought process that will lead you to the key pieces of information you will need as you conduct the negotiation.

PREVIEW YOUR GOALS

I lost count long ago of the number of negotiations in which I participated where the other party was not prepared. The following example illustrates one such negotiation. As often happens when a party is unprepared, the last department manager in the example was unable to adequately express any compelling reasons for implementing his stated goals. See if you can identify the positions that, had she taken some time to preview her goals, would have been defensible.

The rapidly expanding research and development firm I worked for was preparing to move into a new facility. For years, the company had been spread throughout several buildings. One of the major goals was to consolidate the operations of the company into one central location. As part of this transition, the different department managers, who had been strewn across several locations and often separated from key members of their own staffs, had to negotiate for space in the new building.

A committee was formed to design the building and allocate space to the different departments. A meeting was called by the executive team to resolve department space allocation issues. Each department manager had already staked his or her claim in the new layout.

There were only a limited number of offices with windows. On top of that, one of the corporate officers wanted to maximize the amount of light entering the interior of the building. Her solution was to use a modular office concept, with walls only about five feet high, which would allow the light coming in through the outside windows to reach the interior of the building.

The president of the company started the discussion by charting out where the executive offices were to be located. He then told the department managers that everything else was up for grabs, and asked each in turn where he or she might want his or her department located on the new floor plan.

The first department manager, having anticipated the subject of this meeting, had prepared in advance. He began his presentation—complete with a viewgraph presentation—to the assembled group.

* * * * *

"As this viewgraph shows, my department is growing, on average, by 10 employees a year. I anticipate this trend will continue well into the future. To allow for the significant future growth of my department, it is therefore critical that we be located in the part of the building that will allow for maximum staff expansion. Of course, I'm sure that I don't need to remind you that the projects assigned to my department generate the largest share of revenue and income for the company.

"I have studied the layout of the new building and have determined that only one part, the Southwest corner, will be suitable. It is the only location that will allow for the future growth of the department without having to push other groups out, or potentially having to split my department throughout the building as our growth continues."

The next department manager got up and explained her position on the layout of the building:

"As far as I am concerned, modular offices will not be suitable for my department. Each of my employees requires an office with full floor-to-ceiling walls and lockable doors. Since I am in charge of personnel and payroll, my employees are required to handle and store confidential employee data on an ongoing basis.

"This data, which includes salary and other personal information, must be protected. It would be unreasonable to expect my employees to have to secure their information and computers every time they get up from their desks. Aside from the fact that we currently have no plans to buy secured storage containers, it would be very difficult for my employees to take all their information and lock it in a file cabinet just to go to the bathroom. Additionally, unless our computers are kept in locked offices, there is no guarantee that someone who knows what he's doing won't be able to access the employee data."

Finally, the last department manager was asked to explain his plan for the new facility.

"Unfortunately, I really haven't had much time to think about the new building. As you know, I just got back from vacation. Speaking for my staff, we would all definitely prefer to be located in regular offices. I know that my employees will not be happy with modular space. I'm sure that, given a little more time to think about it, I'll be able to come up with at least a few good business reasons, too."

* * * * *

Needless to say, the last department manager is the one who ended up in the modular office space.

While the other managers had foreseen the subject of the meeting, and had determined their positions and rationales in advance, the last department manager came to the meeting completely unprepared. He therefore left the meeting with his real needs unvoiced and unfulfilled.

As this example showed, it's important not only to have goals, but to outline them in advance and be prepared to explain and justify them. In outlining your goals, you want to determine all the items that are up for consideration. One possible goal might be money. How much would you be willing to pay for outside legal services? What's the bottom line for your next raise? How big will your piece of the budget be next year?

The element of time might be an important part of your goals. You may be concerned about when a project starts, when you're going to be promoted, or how long it's going to be before you get transferred to an out-of-state or overseas assignment.

It is important that your goals be set forth in writing in advance of the negotiation. It's not enough that you *think* you have identified all of your goals. Writing your goals down and having them in front of you as you conduct the negotiation, especially in complex situations, will guarantee that you don't inadvertently forget an important point.

It's also a good idea to take the time to brainstorm your goals. Make a list of *every* possible alternative to getting to your desired endpoint. Then take those ideas and whittle them down to the ones which seem most important to meeting your goals.

When you brainstorm, you'll probably end up with many more goals than you'll know what to do with. Pick out the ones that are the most important to you, and list these under the heading "primary goals." Primary goals are those goals that are at the heart of any potential agreement that you plan to negotiate with another party.

Next, establish your secondary goals. Secondary goals are goals that, while you would like to achieve them if at all possible, aren't necessarily critical to the agreement. If your primary goals are not achieved, on the other hand, you would probably not be willing to execute an agreement.

Last, but not least, make a wish list of "dream" goals. Dream goals are those that you don't realistically expect to achieve but that, by listing them along with your primary and secondary goals, you will keep in the back of your mind just in case the opportunity presents itself to pursue them. As you develop trust and a true partnership with your counterpart, dream goals increasingly tend to be converted into reality.

It's best to start with a blank sheet of paper. Write down headings for your primary, secondary, and dream goals. List all of the goals that you feel are non-negotiable under primary, negotiable under secondary, and then your dream goals under the last heading.

The following example shows how you might organize your goals under the three different headings:

GOALS

Primary	*Secondary*	*Dream*
1. _____	_____	_____
2. _____	_____	_____
3. _____	_____	_____
4. _____	_____	_____
5. _____	_____	_____

Let's say that you are preparing to negotiate the terms of a lease for office space for your company. While you know that there is a glut of office space on the market, making the leasing firms particularly anxious to fulfill your terms, you also know that it will still be difficult to find the perfect combination of location, price, and amenities that you are looking for.

As you outline your goals, divide them into the three major categories described above. Under primary goals, indicate the positions that you feel most strongly about. These positions, which may be non-negotiable, might consist of the following:

Primary Goals

1. You may require that the monthly lease payment stay constant throughout the duration of the agreement.

2. You may request a three-year base lease, with two one-year options.

3. You may require that the landlord provide an allowance of up to $50,000 in tenant improvements.

Next, list all of the goals that, while you would like to achieve them if possible, are not critical to reaching an agreement. The secondary goals in this example might include:

Secondary Goals

1. You may attempt to negotiate option-year lease payments at the same rate as the base agreement.
2. You may want the landlord to pay for heating and air conditioning system maintenance for the duration of the agreement.
3. You may want 10 more parking spaces than the lease provides at no extra cost.

Finally, make a list of the goals that you may pursue during the negotiation, but that you don't really expect to achieve. These dream goals might be as follows:

Dream Goals

1. You could request a building buy-out option at the end of the lease.
2. You might request that the landlord amortize tenant improvements beyond the $50,000 allowance over a five-year period.
3. You could request six months free rent as a condition of signing the lease.

When it comes to setting your goals, don't trust them all to memory. Write them down and study them before you embark on your negotiation. You might be surprised at what you will forget to bring up in the heat of discussion. If I had $1 for every goal I have forgotten because I failed to write it down, I would be a rich man, indeed.

RESEARCH THE TOPIC

Good research can turn up information that can be invaluable to your negotiation. When I worked in private industry, I often negotiated contracts with the federal government. Before entering into a negotiation, I always spent time with my project staff to determine what the customer's "hot buttons" might be.

While the media often portrays the federal government as a faceless, monolithic organization that acts and reacts in a very coordinated and uniform manner, this supposition couldn't be farther from the truth. Each government branch, agency, and department is made up of individuals with very different, and often conflicting, goals and agendas.

Some of our customers put schedule or performance above all other priorities. If we were able to guarantee a quick delivery, the customer would be willing to pay almost any price. Other customers might be highly sensitive to the negotiated rate of profit. If we were able to reach a satisfactory agreement on profit, they would be more than happy to agree to a milestone payment schedule that was very advantageous to creating and maintaining a strong positive cash flow.

The point is that every organization and every participant in a negotiation is unique, and each possesses a unique set of goals and priorities. It only takes a little research to reveal your counterpart's goals, constraints, and interests, and to then offer alternatives that are in your mutual interest. It is important to note here that, for every goal you may have, there are many different ways to achieve it.

If you take the time to ask around, you may find out that an employee who works for you has just suffered a financial setback, and that this event may be driving his request for a particular action. With that little bit of information, you can work out a solution that takes mutual needs into account and becomes a win-win outcome for both you and your employee.

When dealing with other companies, you can obtain a lot of valuable information in business magazines such as *Fortune* or *Business Week,* or through reporting services such as Dun & Bradstreet. Annual reports, prospectuses, financial reports, and newspaper articles are also great sources of company information.

You should also find out if anyone in your company has been involved in working out a similar agreement with the same party. This can be a real timesaver. If you can get your hands on any previous agreements, you won't have to waste a lot of time reinventing the wheel. The power of precedence can be a very powerful negotiation tool. By all means, use the power of precedence whenever possible to help you define and reinforce the interests that you share with another party.

When you hear phrases like those that follow, you'll know that your counterpart is trying to influence you to see his point of view by using the power of precedence:

"All of your co-workers have agreed to this new policy. We've worked really hard to make sure that all possible employee concerns have been addressed. Can we count on your support?"

"This is exactly the same-size order as we placed with you last month. Why can't you offer us the same prices? Your costs can't have gone up already."

"Everyone else in the department got a window office . . . even Joe, and Joe is just an account clerk. Don't you think that I deserve a window office, too?"

If a previous agreement is used against you, you don't have to just cave in and accept it. Business is a living, breathing organism that is never exactly the same today as it was yesterday. Yesterday's agreements are just that. The fundamental, baseline assumptions may have changed dramatically since the previous agreement was made. You should therefore never feel constrained by them.

Use previous agreements only if it is in the mutual interest of both you and your counterpart to do so. The power of precedence may be a tremendous aid in defining the boundaries of an agreement. A previous agreement may also be used as the strong foundation on which to construct the framework of a new agreement.

Regardless of how you proceed, it is always best to take stock of your current situation, examine the facts, and ignore previous agreements if they do not directly assist you and your counterpart in finding creative solutions to your requirements.

EVALUATE YOUR COUNTERPART

The primary focus of your research should be to gain a sense of what your counterpart's interests, goals, and concerns might be. You need to develop a certain amount of empathy for his or her position. The more you know about the other party and his or her needs, the more you can anticipate how you counterpart will respond to *your* requests. Additionally, you can better anticipate what positions he will most likely present, and how he will present them.

Try to get a feel for the person you will be negotiating with. Is your counterpart easygoing or intense, patient or fidgety? Is he introverted and hard to draw out, or extroverted and hard to control? Does your counterpart have a sense of humor, or does he or she lack passion? Does she express herself well, or does she make her points only with great difficulty? The answers to these questions, and others like them, will make a very significant difference in how you go about your negotiation.

If your counterpart is aggressive and demanding, you will want to calmly, but firmly, state your goals and explore your mutual interests. If you show an aggressive counterpart that you cannot be easily bullied into a win-lose situation, he will be much more likely to work with you to find mutually agreeable alternatives and solutions.

If, on the other hand, your counterpart is passive and uncommunicative, you will have to take charge and draw him out of his shell. Make a special effort to discover what your counterpart's goals are, and what alternatives might be acceptable in meeting them.

You should also take the time to try to identify the person's motivations. What does he have to gain or lose in his dealings with you? Which of your requests will elicit a yawn of boredom, and which will cause the other party to explode through the roof and into orbit? What kind of stake does your counterpart have in the final agreement? Is she desperate to reach agreement, or could she care less?

As you negotiate, gauge the reactions of the other party. If you are observant, you will be able to compare his or her words with the nonverbal messages that are also being communicated. It is an established fact that nonverbal messages make up the majority of our overall communication. The astute negotiator will be on the lookout for the nonverbal messages that contradict a person's words. Someone might say, for example, that he is open to further negotiation, while taking on a closed-arm stance that flashes: "I have made up my mind!"

Some topics are not subject to negotiation. Several years ago, when I negotiated contracts with IBM, their proprietary information agreements contained such a non-negotiable clause. If you wanted to work on a project with IBM, and most companies would have jumped at the chance, you were required to execute the standard agreement.

The catch was a clause in the agreement that allowed IBM to use the other parties' proprietary information in any way they wished, as long as IBM did not disclose it outside of the company. The proprietary information could be used for marketing, product development, or whatever purpose they deemed necessary. It was commonly known that IBM would not negotiate this clause. They might entertain minor revisions to some of the words, but the essence of the clause was non-negotiable.

By knowing your opposition, you won't have to waste a lot of time in situations where a certain term or condition is not negotiable. You may find, however, that you can use that fact as leverage, especially if you have to give up some tremendous rights in order to reach an agreement. If that's the case, then use the leverage to make sure that you get concessions on other parts of the agreement.

After you have thoroughly researched the topics and have begun to get a sense of your opposition, you will also begin to anticipate the positions and responses of the other party during the negotiation process. There may be some obvious responses that you can anticipate.

For example, if you are in a situation where you are asking for a budget increase for next year, you might anticipate the following questions:

"The company is getting ready to cut another 500 jobs. There must be alternatives that you can explore besides a budget increase. Have you considered other options?"

"Can you justify each and every dollar you've asked for?"

"Before I can approve an increase in the expense side of your budget, can you show me comparable increases in the revenue side of your budget?

Once you have solved a particular problem, you will likely be able to recognize it the next time you see it coming. After you have worked through the same problem a few times, you should be able to anticipate the questions that your counterpart is going to ask:

In this manner, you will be able to prepare your responses to your counterpart's anticipated goals or positions. Mentally run through as many different scenarios as possible before you start the negotiation. You can anticipate his requests, rehearse his positions, and act through your responses, well before you ever face the individual.

Remember, your primary reason for making the effort to anticipate your counterpart's goals and interests is to be able to identify and act on the goals and interests that you both have in common. Through this process of investigation and discovery, you can ensure that, when the negotiation is complete, you will both be winners.

PREPARE YOUR RATIONALE

As you outline your goals, you should also consider how you will defend them. It is not enough to say "I have a goal, and I think you should agree to it because it will be in our mutual interests to do so." No, if you are going to convince someone that it is in his interest to go along with your request, you have got to tell him why.

Several years ago, I was negotiating a deal for the acquisition of new office copying equipment with a representative from a well-known Fortune 500 corporation. See if you can understand why I was less than anxious to go out of my way to grant the salesman's request.

* * * * *

"Thanks for agreeing to meet with me today, Peter. I never thought that we would get this deal wrapped up, but it looks like we're just about there. I have brought a list of outstanding issues with me—don't worry, the list is fairly short. Do you want to go through yours first?"

"No problem, Kirk. Why don't you go through your list first? We have already agreed on the system configurations, prices, and delivery. What else is there to discuss?"

This deal *had* been a long time in the making. Our current office copiers had gone well beyond the point of obsolescence several years before we reached this point. Fortunately, corporate management had finally grown weary of the constant complaints by managers whose last-minute, rush proposals were eaten by the perpetually hungry machinery, or whose secretaries had threatened to quit if they had to fish one more piece of paper out of the jammed innards of the toner-laden monsters.

"Well, Peter, there is just one minor item that I need to get your approval on. You know that we made every effort to give you the very best prices possible on the systems. We were even able to set up financing for the deal."

"Sure, I really appreciate the extra effort that you expended to meet our budgetary constraints. As you know, we went through an exhaustive technical review and selection process to determine which brand of office copiers would best meet our needs. Your line of copiers stood heads and shoulders above the rest of the pack."

"Thanks for your confidence in our products. Now, I hope you will be able to help *me* out. I know that you aren't planning to execute a purchase order until next month."

"That's right, Kirk. I still have to get the approval of our chief financial officer, since this deal is well above my level of signature authority. I think we should plan to give her enough time to review the file thoroughly."

"That's my problem. Our fiscal year ends on the 30th of this month. I really need to get the machines installed this month so the sale will be credited this fiscal year. I'm in the running for an all-expenses-paid vacation to Hawaii. This sale should put me over the top. Can't you get me the purchase order before the end of the month?"

"I just don't see how I can, Kirk. I definitely don't want to rush Susan—you know what a stickler she can be. Besides, the old copiers aren't going to be removed by the vendor until the 15th of next month. The rooms are already crowded enough as it is. We don't even have the circuits rewired yet to handle the extra load that your machines are going to put on them. How are our employees going to get their work done?"

"It would only be for a couple of weeks, at the most. Don't you think you could do just this one favor for me?"

"I don't know, Kirk. I frankly don't see what your proposal buys us."

* * * * *

As can be seen in the above situation, Kirk had not prepared adequately for this negotiation session and was therefore unlikely to succeed. He had not thoroughly researched the needs of his customer, and he did not have an acceptable rationale for his position. Finally, Kirk had not anticipated the needs of his customer, and he did not have well-developed solutions to the stated problems. Had Kirk been better prepared, he might have responded in the following way:

* * * * *

"I know that Susan is going to need plenty of time to review the paperwork, Peter. I don't want to give you the impression that I am pressuring you. However, there are some very definite advantages you should know about if you accept delivery of the copiers before the end of the month."

"Like what, Kirk."

"Well, aside from the fact that you'll get the immediate benefit of our trouble-free, low-maintenance copiers, which will make a lot of people in this building very happy, we're offering a special promotion to our large-volume customers. If you take delivery of your order before the 30th of this month, we can give you, absolutely free, a brand new model 300xt desktop copier to be used as you please."

"Hmmmm . . . that sounds like a pretty attractive offer. Let me see if I can't get Susan to approve the purchase order today? I'll call our current vendor and see if we can't accelerate the removal of the in-place equipment. While I do that, maybe our maintenance staff can take a look at the circuits. I'm sure we'll be able to work this out."

* * * * *

As the above example shows, just a little preparation (and, in this case, the ability to offer a tangible incentive to the other party) can go a long way in helping you meet your goals. Instead of coming away from the negotiation with nothing to show for his efforts but a bruised ego, Kirk presented a compelling reason for Peter to accelerate the execution of a purchase order—one that likely will ensure that Kirk will meet his goal of getting the equipment in place before the end of the month.

If you seriously expect to get the things you want from someone, you clearly must have a well thought-out rationale prepared in advance. Not only must your rationale be well thought-out, but it must address the interests and goals of your counterpart.

If you are only interested in having your own goals fulfilled, you will have a very tough time trying to sell your agenda. No one likes to deal with a person who only has his own interests in mind when negotiating. Always keep your counterpart's interests at the forefront of your own agenda. You'll be much more successful if you do.

WORKSHEETS

The PREP system can be a very powerful tool to help you achieve your goals in a negotiation. Ask yourself the following questions as you apply the PREP system to your own particular situation.

Preview Your Goals

What are your primary goals?

_____

_____

_____

_____

What are your secondary goals?

_____

_____

_____

_____

What are your dream goals?

_____

_____

_____

_____

Research the Topic

What were the terms and conditions of previous, similar agreements?

_____

_____

_____

_____

_____

What sources of information are available regarding this customer?

_____

_____

_____

_____

_____

Evaluate Your Counterpart

What are your counterpart's personality traits and inner motivations?

_____

_____

_____

_____

_____

What does the other party have to gain in this negotiation?

_____

_____

_____

_____

_____

What does the other party have to lose in this negotiation?

_____

_____

_____

_____

_____

What objections can you expect in response to your requests?

_____

_____

_____

_____

_____

What are your counterpart's interests and goals?

_____

_____

_____

_____

_____

How will your counterpart defend his interests and goals?

_____

_____

_____

_____

_____

Prepare Your Rationale

Exactly why do you not need to achieve your specific goals?

_____

_____

_____

_____

_____

What would happen if you were not able to achieve your goals?

_____

_____

_____

_____

_____

What does your counterpart have to gain by agreeing to your goals?

_____

_____

_____

_____

_____

What does your counterpart have to lose by agreeing to your goals?

_____

_____

_____

_____

_____

List the aspects of your plan that benefit both parties.

_____

_____

_____

_____

_____

Chapter Five

Where to Start?

No task is a long one but the task on which one dare not start. It becomes a nightmare.

Charles Baudelaire

How you begin your negotiation depends on many different factors. The approach you choose to reach an agreement with an employee on her work schedule will be much different than the approach you would choose to sell a client on a multimillion dollar deal. So too will your approach, and the setting in which you choose to conduct it, depend on the particulars of your unique circumstance.

The primary goal at the outset is to effectively communicate your interests and goals to the other party. Of course, to ensure that a final agreement meets the needs of both parties, receiving and acknowledging your counterpart's goals and interests are just as important as the transmission of your goals and interests. Additionally, as a critical part of the communication process, you must make every effort to ensure that you are speaking to a person who has the authority to make a decision.

In exploring the subtleties of kicking-off a negotiation, we will learn how to identify authority, how to present positions, and how to describe our limits and goals. Finally, we will spend some time discussing the proper selection of a negotiation approach.

RECOGNIZING AUTHORITY

I was preparing to call a potential customer concerning a proposal that we had prepared and submitted several weeks earlier. At that time, my counterpart seemed to be very interested in our proposal, and indicated that she would be able to act on it in the very near future.

The proposal, which would provide work for a large portion of our staff, was very important to my company's continued financial well-being. After politely waiting for her to get back to me about the proposal, I decided that enough time had passed and that it was time to get the negotiation off the ground.

* * * * *

"Krista? This is Peter Economy. How are you doing today?"

"Oh, I'm fine. I'm up to my ears in alligators, as usual. You know, nothing new there."

"That's good to hear. I would hate for you to get bored."

I had been dealing with Krista for several months—ever since she started her new job. Although our contracts to date were for relatively low dollar amounts, I wasn't aware of anything that might limit Krista's ability to negotiate and execute any manner of agreement.

"I just wanted to see if you are ready to start the negotiation on our proposal. You probably noticed that the proposed start date is in just two weeks. That will allow us to get the final product to your technical guys in time for the test program."

"Yeah. I was hoping to get around to it soon, Peter. Let me take a close look at it. I'll call you back by the end of the week."

Although pushing the start of negotiations to the end of the week meant that we would have only one week to negotiate and execute the agreement, I was confident that Krista would make every effort to follow through on her promise.

I was under considerable pressure from both the program manager and our chief financial officer. The program manager wanted to ensure that he had a direct charge number available to keep 15 relatively high-paid members of his staff off of group overhead, and the chief financial officer wanted to make sure that we started the project on schedule to minimize any potential negative cash flow.

Finally, on Wednesday of the following week, Krista and I were able to reach an agreement on all of the contract terms and conditions. We were both pleased that we had arrived at a solution that satisfied both of our interests. Our customer would get a quality product at a reasonable price, and we would keep a talented group of employees on our payroll for another year, while making a reasonable profit for our efforts. I was, of course, anxious to get a formal authorization to proceed from Krista.

"So now that we're in agreement, let's discuss the details of contract execution so we can stay on schedule. If you can send the contract to me tonight, I can sign it tomorrow and return it to you tomorrow night. That way, you'll have it on your desk for your signature by 10:30 Friday morning. Just fax me the cover page and we'll do the rest."

"I'm sorry to tell you this, Peter, but I'll have to get the formal endorsement of the contract review board before I can send the contract out for your signature."

"Contract review board?"

"Yeah, my signature authority is limited to $1 million. Everything above that level is forwarded directly to the contract review board for approval. I won't be able to give you an authorization to proceed until the board approves the deal."

"You know how important it is that we get started, Krista. If we don't get started on Friday, I can't guarantee that we'll be able to meet your scheduled test dates. When does the contract review board meet again? This week? Next week?"

"Give me a minute to check my calendar, Peter. Let's see . . . they met last Friday. According to my schedule, their next meeting is three weeks from this Friday."

* * * * *

I had run into one of the most critical and frustrating stumbling blocks in the negotiation process—the lack of real authority to negotiate or consummate a deal.

At best, I would find myself without an executed agreement for the more than three weeks that it would take for formal approval of the agreement. At worst, I could find, at the end of the three weeks, that the contract review board might overrule Krista, thus further delaying or even rejecting the start of the project. Either way, failure to identify authority and its limits early in the negotiation was a critical error that could waste countless hours and cause a good deal to go bad.

The first way to identify your counterpart's authority is to attempt to gain the necessary information during the preparation and research phases of the negotiation.

If your counterpart is within your own company, you will easily be able to find out the person's position and limits of authority. You can, for example, find out what budget authority he may have; what authority he may have to execute checks or purchase orders; what supervisory or managerial responsibilities he has; and other information that would give you an empirical basis to determine the limits of your counterpart's authority.

If your counterpart cannot agree to your goals because of some limitation in his authority, you may have jump to the next higher level in the chain of command to achieve them. As a part of your research, you should also find out who that person is.

If the other party is external to your organization, you can still find ways to research his level of authority before you enter into the negotiation. Of course, this will be much more difficult than it would be if the person was inside your organization.

You may be able to obtain information about these external parties from other people within your own company, external contacts, or through documents such as annual reports or company brochures. Alternatively, a method that I've found works wonders is to make a blind call to the company receptionist and start asking questions.

Another way to define authority is to ask your counterpart outright if he has the authority to finalize the deal. Since this approach could be misconstrued by your counterpart as a personal affront to his position or status, you must be particularly careful not to offend him. If you have not been successful in your research prior to the start of the negotiation, go ahead and ask that person what his limits are.

I have found simple, direct questions to be quite effective in helping to determine a counterpart's limits:

"Can you authorize this change in the personnel policy, or do we have to get someone else's blessing, too?"

"Do you have the authority to sign purchase orders of any amount for your company?"

"Can you make the final decision, or are you going to have to call your corporate headquarters to get the authorization to solve my problem?"

Most people who have been granted authority also have limits placed upon that authority. This is generally true with everyone you will be negotiating with. Try to find out whether your counterpart possesses the authority to negotiate and approve the deal at hand, and exactly what his limits of authority are.

Is he limited in the amount of money that he is allowed to commit for the company? $1,000, $10,000, $100,000, or $1 million?

Is he limited by the jurisdiction of the potential agreement? For example, does he handle all of the franchises in the Northeast region of the United States, but have no authority to negotiate franchises in the rest of the country? Or, can your counterpart make programmatic decisions at the group level, but not at the corporate level?

It bears repeating: before you start a negotiation, set aside some time to determine the limits of your counterpart's authority. What would normally be a quick and easy negotiation can easily die on the vine if you are not negotiating with the right person.

REVISITING YOUR OBJECTIVES

Remember the list of goals that you developed in the previous chapter? Before the negotiation starts, you must become intimately familiar with them. Which objectives are most important to you? Which are least important? Which goals are most important to your counterpart? Which are least important? How do your goals mesh with those of your counterpart? Can you find any common ground?

If you went through the process of arranging your goals into primary, secondary, and dream categories, it will be fairly easy for you to prioritize your objectives. On the other hand, if you have not yet made a list of your objectives, do it now!

Don't forget to consider your indirect objectives as well as your direct objectives. Let's say that an employee has approached you to see if you would be willing to waive a company policy. While you may not have a major concern with a one-time exception to the rules, you may feel that this issue deserves further consideration.

Your direct primary and secondary goals in this situation might include maintaining strict adherence to corporate policies, allowing for flexibility to account for personal situations, or getting something in return from the employee, such as a promise to work on a holiday. Indirect objectives, although not a part of the final agreement, should also be considered. Such indirect goals might include your desire to keep the employee's morale up, a need to draw the line because of some employee transgression, or the desire to be perceived as a consensus-building team player.

If you take a close look at these indirect objectives—often called the "hidden agenda"—you may discover much of the motivation behind the direct goals on your explicit agenda. This knowledge may lead you to reconsider your goals and either change priorities or exchange these goals for other, more important ones.

While you may gain significant insights into your goals, or your counterpart's goals, by considering the impact of indirect objectives, it is important not to lose sight of the primary, motivating interests that really drive a negotiation. Keep these mutual interests front and center on your agenda as you negotiate.

A FORMULA FOR AGREEMENT

With all the knowledge that we have gained thus far in our discussion, we can establish an empirical formula for a negotiated agreement in relatively short order.

The most effective formula for agreement will be nothing more than a compilation of all the data that you have gathered, organized, and sequenced in an ordered fashion. The constants and variables in your particular formula are merely the combination of your goals, limits, research, and rationale. Each individual negotiation will have its own unique formula for agreement. The challenge in any negotiation is to achieve rough parity between the parties of the negotiation as follows:

$$\text{Goals}_1 + \text{Limits}_1 \cong \text{Goals}_2 + \text{Limits}_2$$

This formula simply represents the situation where the goals and limitations of the first person or group are roughly in balance with the goals and limitations of the second person or group.

Unless one of the parties is under financial or emotional duress, it is unlikely that agreement will be reached until both sides of the equation are perceived to be in balance by all participants. It should always be your goal to achieve parity, or a win-win situation, in all of your negotiations. While true parity, or a 100 percent win-win situation, takes hard work to achieve, the fact is that every agreement offers the opportunity—if you are willing to look hard enough to find it.

The above formula defines what is known as a "win-win" outcome. Clearly, an agreement where all parties gain on a relatively equal basis is preferable to the situation where one party wins and the other party loses. Not only are win-win outcomes preferable in business, they are essential for the fostering of long-term business relationships.

The days when businesspeople can assert victory by creating losers are, hopefully, behind us. I sincerely believe that there are only two types of negotiation outcomes: win-win and no-win. If both parties don't win, then both parties have lost.

The reason that the concept of win-win negotiation is so popular nowadays is that most managers realize that, to ensure long-term stability in an organization or relationship, it is best that all parties to a negotiation fulfill as many of their goals as possible. The enlightened businessperson further realizes that, if an agreement is forced on another party through duress, the ultimate agreement reached will be unstable due to resentment on the part of the losing party.

This interpersonal instability can be represented mathematically by the formula shown below. In this case, the first party has "won" the negotiation; the second party has "lost."

$$Goals_1 + Limits_1 > Goals_2 + Limits_2$$

This situation is inherently unstable. It is a basic law of nature that, when one side of a chemical equation is predominant over the other, there will be a strong tendency for the sides to seek equilibrium. People who have been forced into a losing situation will also seek their own equilibrium. The loser will try to recover what he or she has lost—one way or another. Unfortunately, the methods that the loser chooses to apply may be counterproductive to the party who thinks he has won.

It's not too hard to imagine a situation where the party who has lost will try to become a winner, potentially at great cost to the so-called winning party. I recall, for example, when the employees' union at a major airline was forced to accept major labor concessions by company management several years ago. After the negotiation was complete and management had declared itself the "winner," I'm sure that the executives were quite jubilant about their hard-won victory. At least, that is, until the pilots started to call in sick.

For some undetermined reason, there was an instantaneous and widespread epidemic among the airline's pilots, copilots, and flight engineers. This epidemic, along with its resultant negative impact on the most critical element of the workforce, led to flight cancellations, arrival and departure delays, and a lot of irate customers.

It didn't take long for the national news media to pick up on these events and broadcast them throughout the nation. Passengers quickly sought other airlines for their air travel needs.

The victory that management had savored only weeks before, suddenly didn't seem quite so sweet.

There are many different ways a loser can try to make up for his loss. Even if the loss is not substantial, the losing party may feel a need to reach parity, if only to save face with co-workers or peers. Hurt pride or a bruised ego can often be more important to a person than an actual loss of wages or benefits.

That's why the concept of win-win negotiation is so important in business. While the losers you create may not succeed in reaching their goals today, they will definitely try to make up their losses sometime in the future. In business, we have enough to worry about without having to control the instability that win-lose negotiations create.

PRESENTING YOUR PROPOSALS

We are finally ready to start our negotiation! If you've followed my advice so far, you have probably prepared, prepared, and prepared some more until you can't stand it any longer. Now it's time to make things happen.

The more critical the topic is to the fundamental viability of your business, the more probable it is that you will want to be highly formalized in your approach. A formal presentation tends to lend weight to your arguments. I'm sure you've observed the difference in your employees' attentiveness when you approach them very formally and seriously with an issue, in contrast to a light-hearted informal approach.

In the following example, the sales representative of an office equipment manufacturer presented my company with a proposal to replace outmoded data terminals with a local area network and personal computers.

* * * * *

"Has everyone had a chance to read our proposal?"

"Yes—speaking for the group—we have all studied your proposal in great detail. I know I have some specific questions that need to be answered before we go much further."

"I can understand that you might have some questions, Peter, and I think that we should explore them fully. At this point, however, I believe it would be best to go through the elements of the proposal point by point, and then see what questions remain."

"Okay—I'll buy that."

"The keys points of our proposal are enumerated on page five. We consider these items to be reasonable and critical to successful completion of this project. To begin, we propose to give you a generous allowance of $4,500 for your old equipment. As you know, the equipment is just about obsolete. You will find that this amount is substantially better than you could do on the open market. It will take two weeks to make the complete transition, including installation and training on the new equipment."

"That all sounds well and good, but how are we going to get any work done while you guys are playing around with these new computers?"

"I'm glad you asked that question. For no extra charge, we will complete the full installation over the weekend. You'll all go home Friday evening, and return Monday morning to find a complete, networked system ready to go to work for you. This will allow office production to go on with a minimum of disruption."

"Okay—so far so good. What's the bottom line?"

"To do all the things we've outlined in our proposal— remove the old equipment, check out and deliver the new 486 network server and personal computers to your facility, run the cable, set up the hardware, install the selected software, put all the units through a complete and final checkout, and then train up to five selected employees on how to operate the equipment—we have worked up a total price of $32,500. We can commit to complete delivery and installation two weeks after we sign the contract. Upon approval of your credit application, we will be willing to offer net/30 payment terms. I believe you will find that most of our competitors require 50 percent down before they will start work. I have all the contracts right here. Are you ready to make a commitment today?"

* * * * *

While the above formal presentation was specifically geared to the sale of new computer equipment, many of the techniques can be applied in any negotiation situation.

The sales representative has clearly and concisely presented all of his goals to his counterpart. While he has not told his customer which of his goals are primary, secondary, or dream, they are all an integral part of this proposal. The sales representative thoroughly prepared in advance and knows exactly what he wants to achieve. He also knows that he has room to maneuver to ensure that he gets the order.

The sales representative also has a firm knowledge of his limits. He has already worked up the numbers for a variety of scenarios. Since the buyer is unlikely to accept the initial offer without trying to negotiate the price down or modify some of the other terms, the sales representative has already allowed for ample flexibility in achieving his goals while helping his customer achieve his goals.

He has researched his competition and is familiar with the ways they do business. He knows their prices. He keeps abreast of their new product introductions. He follows up with customers who have decided to do business with his competitors, and finds out why they made their decisions. The sales representative brings all this information with him to the presentation, and he is ready to work it into the discussion.

Finally, the sales representative has anticipated his customer's responses, and prepared a rationale to support his requests.

Most of our day-to-day negotiations are not as structured and formal as the one described in the above example. Instead, these daily negotiations are typically quite informal. An employee approaches you to establish a flexible work schedule. You call the facilities manager to get the air conditioner in your office fixed. Your secretary is going to be late putting together the report that's due to the board of directors on Friday.

Just because these less-formal negotiations are not as structured—with a defined agenda, full-color glossy briefing package, and viewgraphs—does not mean that you should be any less prepared.

RECEIVING THEIR PROPOSALS

At some point in your deliberations, you will be presented with proposals or counterproposals from the other party. Be prepared to receive them. In any process that involves communication between two individuals, it is as important to listen effectively as it is to effectively transmit your message in the first place.

When receiving the other party's proposals, shift into an active listening mode. Let no part of the proposal escape your attention. Too often I have seen parties arguing over points that one participant thought the other had put forward when, in fact, no such points had been proposed.

In the following example, I was seeking authorization from my human resources department to hire a temporary employee for a few days. Johanna, our human resources manager, and I actively listened to each other during the course of our negotiation—primarily because we both had a vested interest in the outcome.

* * * * *

"So what do you say, Johanna? I need to get a temp lined up by the end of the week so we can train him to fill in for Bob. Can I count on you to help me out?"

Only one week before, Bob had been transferred to my department. I assumed that, along with Bob, a budget allocation would be transferred from his old department to cover the expense. I would now be responsible for his payroll and ancillary costs, including temporary support when Bob was absent. I figured that the budget transfer was a given.

"Give me a minute to check your budget first, Peter. Before I do, however, remind me how many hours you think you'll need the temp. I can't remember what you said before."

"I figure that, including a half-day for training, we'll need the temp for a total of 20 hours."

"Okay—20 hours total? Let me see what you can afford."

Johanna leafed through the bulky computer printout. Occasionally, she tapped out a few numbers on the keys of her calculator.

"Hmmm . . . it looks like we have a problem, Peter."

"What kind of problem, Johanna?"

"Well, it appears that you have already overrun your temporary employee budget for the year. I double-checked the numbers and I'm still coming up with the same result."

"How could I have overrun the budget? I know that I am running pretty tight against my original fiscal-year budget but, since I picked up responsibility for Bob from your department last week, I should have plenty of room to maneuver. What was the total increase in my temporary employee budget line as a result of Bob transferring over?"

"What increase? I didn't transfer any funding for temporary employee services to your department, Peter."

"What do you mean, you didn't transfer any funds? If you transferred the employee, you've got to transfer the dollars to support him, too."

"I'm sorry, Peter, but I barely have enough funding to take care of my staff, much less transferring any to your department."

"That's not going to be acceptable, Johanna. I have got to have the funding to support Bob. You budgeted for Bob this year. The money should come from your budget!"

"No. I'm not going to let go of a single penny. You're just going to have to work it out on your own."

"Did you hear what I said, Johanna? You budgeted for him originally—the money is still in your budget. You can't just transfer Bob without transferring the funding to support him."

"Fine, Peter! I'll see what I can do."

* * * * *

To be successful in any business negotiation situation, you have to receive and understand the other person's proposals with an efficiency that approaches 100 percent. Be an active listener! Don't let anything escape your notice or block your channels of communication.

For successful communication to occur, two basic things have to happen. The first thing that has to happen is that the original message must be transmitted effectively. The second thing that has to happen is that the original message, assuming that it has been transmitted effectively, must be received just as effectively.

So, how can you help correct a situation where the message has not been effectively transmitted? You can question the other party to find out exactly what points she is trying to communicate. If you are uncertain about an exact point she has made or position she has taken, ask her to clarify the position or point.

After you have fully received the proposals and feel that you understand all of the points, restate the position and ask the other party to confirm it. Only after your repetition has been confirmed should you proceed with a negotiation. Otherwise, you'll waste precious time making sure that all parties are working from the same sheet of music.

DEFINING YOUR LIMITATIONS

So far, we have progressed through the process of presenting and receiving proposals. It might not be a bad idea, at this point, to take the time to present your goals and limitations to the other party. While you are clearly under no obligation to do so, it may help to accelerate the negotiation process. It is unquestionably a good idea to get your limitations on the table as early in the process as possible.

Limitations are nothing more than the boundaries of a potential agreement. Limitations define the extent to which we are willing to be flexible in our goals.

If you do not allow for flexibility in your proposals, you will find it difficult for the other party to see any reason to agree to your goals. If you fix your positions in concrete early in a negotiation, you will also solidify your counterpart's positions. Flexibility in your proposals will allow for flexibility in your counterpart's proposals.

A real time-waster is the process by which we attempt to uncover unvoiced limitations. It's like walking around your house in the dark and running into obstacles that you can't see. Turn on the light, and your obstacles are suddenly illuminated and your path is clear. Similarly, you have to find ways to illuminate your counterpart's obstacles. Once the obstacles have been revealed, you can both focus on solutions that meet your mutual goals.

It can be very frustrating when limitations are kept hidden. You may think that the key issues have been resolved, only to find that you're not able to reach an agreement due to some vague reasons that can't be pinpointed.

You've no doubt been in situations where you just didn't understand why you couldn't reach agreement with your counterpart on a particular issue. One weak excuse or another may have been voiced as a reason for the reticence, but you have a gut feeling that there's something else at issue. If you knew what the real reason was, you might be able to come to an agreement by getting past this hidden issue.

By no means am I suggesting that you should reveal *all* your secrets to your counterpart. I *am* saying that you should fully describe your real limitations early in the negotiation process. A negotiation will be much more effective if both parties know and can negotiate within established parameters or boundaries.

The following example shows how two parties defined the outline of their limitations early in the negotiation process, by describing the parameters within which they could negotiate. This particular situation occurred at an off-site manager's meeting called to discuss serious morale problems within the organization.

* * * * *

"Okay, everyone. Let's get started. I know it's early in the morning, but I want to make some definite progress before we break for lunch."

Margaret was in a very difficult position. The chairman of the board of directors fired Margaret's predecessor only six months earlier. The former chief executive, George, was much loved and universally respected by all employees, management and staff included. Unfortunately, he spoke his mind a few times too often, and ran afoul of the board. As a result, Margaret inherited a disgruntled workforce that was not at all shy about expressing displeasure with the status quo.

"I asked each of you to poll your employees to find out what the significant morale issues are. If we are going to build a high-performing team here, we have to get to the heart of these problems and solve them. Yes, John. Do you have a question?"

"I was just wondering if there are any limits on what we can bring forward for consideration, Margaret. Some of the members of my staff spoke to me very candidly about their personal concerns about our management team. I'm afraid that some of the managers in this room might feel personally affronted by some of these concerns."

"No, John. I want us to be able to talk straight with each other in this meeting. If our employees have problems with the way that we as managers do business, it's in everyone's interest to hear about it—no matter who is at fault. We may or may not agree with their assessment, but we should at least address their concerns.

"Now, don't get me wrong, there are some topics that we just aren't going to be able to satisfactorily resolve, at least not in the current environment, so I don't want to waste our time discussing them. Now, what have you come up with? Cindy?"

"I was frankly surprised, Margaret, to find out how dissatisfied some members of my staff are about things. They mentioned the ongoing lack of trust between management and staff, the problems with our facility, specifically the poor air quality, and poor communications. The biggest morale issue by far, however, is the alternate work schedule. As you know, the previous chief executive promised the employees that we would implement an alternate work schedule program this fiscal year."

"Now, that's what I am talking about, Cindy. The alternate work schedule is not on the table for consideration. The board of directors has already determined, unequivocally, that we will not implement that particular program. We can just forget it. The other morale problems you brought up—the trust issue, the facility, poor communications—we can discuss solutions to those issues at today's meeting."

* * * * *

In the above situation, the parties have worked out some basic parameters within which they will be willing to work. Margaret is serious about addressing the staff morale issues. She feels that, regardless of whose feelings are hurt, all the issues should be brought forward.

On the other hand, by defining some issues as off-limits, Margaret has negotiated a range of consideration with the management team. All the players now understand the rules, and can work effectively within the proscribed limitations.

As you outline your goals, simultaneously define your limits. What are the minimum and maximum boundaries of an agreement? What would happen if one of your priority goals is not reached? Would you really give up the negotiation and refuse to settle? Or would you be willing to concede that goal in the interest of reaching a final agreement?

The answers to these questions will ultimately determine where you will end up. Negotiations are conducted on the presumption that there will be give and take on both sides. This give-and-take process prescribes that each party will be willing to give up some goals to reach an agreement. Both parties must therefore know the limits of their positions.

You have to ask yourself: "What is really important to me and what is not? Which goals are hard, and which ones would I be willing to give up as part of the negotiation process?"

You also have to ask yourself: "What are my counterpart's goals, and how can I help him achieve his goals while he helps me achieve mine? How can we both come out of this negotiation as winners?"

Each party to a negotiation will have his own range of negotiable positions. These ranges will generally overlap. If the ranges do not overlap, there will be no common ground for reaching an agreement. Fortunately, in most negotiations, the ranges do overlap. Sometimes, when the ranges do not overlap, one party or the other is willing to extend his range to reach agreement. What you may perceive as a non-negotiable item at the beginning of a negotiation may become a negotiable item by the end.

Many times I have been involved in negotiations where hard-and-fast positions were discussed early on. As both parties got farther into the negotiation, and as concessions were made by both sides, positions that were previously cast in concrete became more flexible. The give-and-take process, along with the overriding interest of both parties in reaching an agreement, brought about this flexibility in previously inflexible positions.

DECIDING ON AN APPROACH

Let's say that you have outlined your goals, determined your limits, researched the topic, and begun to know your opposition. You have also anticipated your opponent's responses, prepared your rationale, and researched your counterpart's interests. It is now time to select the approach you will take to open the negotiation.

There are as many different ways to start a negotiation as there are stars in the sky. The approach that you select, however, will ultimately determine your success. Select the right approach, and you may be surprised at how quickly you reach your objectives. Select the wrong approach, and you'll need all the help you can get. Be careful in selecting an initial approach. The opening round often sets the tone for the entire negotiation.

Since we can't always be fortunate enough to have chosen the best approach from the outset, the key to long-term success is to be *flexible*. Tailor your approach to the situation. Be prepared with a wide variety of alternatives and solutions. Above all, keep the interests of your counterpart in mind as you explore the possibilities for agreement. If you are persistent enough, you'll eventually find an approach that does the trick.

While we can agree here that a cooperatively negotiated agreement is best for both parties, there will be times when you will face an opponent who thinks that a cooperative negotiation is one where you cooperate with each and every one of his demands. In this kind of situation, you will have to be prepared to defend your own interests. Since your opponent isn't interested in a win-win outcome, the responsibility will rest with you.

In general, when starting a negotiation and selecting an approach, it's most prudent to choose an approach that is neutral—neither too aggressive nor too passive. You will want to be firm in your approach, and sincere, but not overbearing. At the same time, you will want to be receptive to your counterpart's interests and not turn him off by being too aggressive, or mislead him into taking an aggressive approach when he perceives that you cannot defend your own interests.

The key to selecting your approach is flexibility. Although you may select an initial approach, you must be able to modify it at any time during the course of the negotiation. Only by maintaining flexibility will you be able to assure that you successfully meet your goals, while helping your counterpart meet his goals.

WORKSHEETS

There are many different ways to start a negotiation. How you start a particular negotiation depends on the unique factors of your individual situation. Before you select your approach, review the following checklists as an aid in identifying the key factors that will influence the successful commencement of your negotiation.

Recognizing Authority

It's important that you take the time to identify the limits of your counterpart's authority. Doing so will ensure that your efforts are targeted to the right person.

- ❏ Identify your counterpart's authority.
- ❏ Determine your counterpart's limitations.
- ❏ Identify your counterpart's next-level supervisor.
- ❏ Ask the other party to describe his limitations.
- ❏ Don't assume that your counterpart has unlimited authority.

Revisiting Your Objectives

As you prepared for the negotiation, you developed a list of your primary, secondary, and dream goals. Before starting the negotiation, take a few minutes to review them again.

- ❏ Review your goals and objectives.
- ❏ Prioritize your goals and objectives.
- ❏ Consider indirect as well as direct objectives.
- ❏ Does your counterpart have a hidden agenda?
- ❏ Revise your goals and priorities as necessary.

A Formula for Agreement

Unbalanced agreements are unstable agreements. The best agreements are balanced, win-win agreements. Balanced agreements tend to be stable, and therefore long-term in nature.

- ❑ Compile and sequence your goals, limits, research, and rationale.
- ❑ Determine the relative equity of your positions versus your counterpart's.
- ❑ Define an equitable, win-win formula for agreement.
- ❑ Avoid unbalanced, and hence unstable, agreements.
- ❑ Consider long-term relationships over short-term exigencies.
- ❑ Create winning, not losing, partners.

Presenting Your Proposals

Presentations can, depending on the situation, range from completely informal to highly formal. Regardless of the formality of your presentation, be prepared to clearly communicate your goals and rationale to the other party.

- ❑ Assess the formality of the situation.
- ❑ Clearly and concisely present your goals to the other party.
- ❑ Know your limits.
- ❑ Know your counterpart's limits.
- ❑ Be prepared to provide rationales to support your goals and interests.

Receiving Their Proposals

Just as it is important to be effective in presenting your positions, it is just as important to listen to and understand your counterpart's goals.

- ❑ Focus your undivided attention on your counterpart's proposals.
- ❑ Utilize active listening techniques.
- ❑ Confirm your understandings with the other party.
- ❑ If in doubt, ask your counterpart to clarify your understandings.

Defining Your Limitations

While not mandatory, it is often helpful to define your limitations for the other party. Instead of wasting time on dead-end avenues, you can concentrate on solutions that will be acceptable to all parties.

- ❑ Present your goals and limitations to the other party.
- ❑ Allow for flexibility in your proposals.
- ❑ Attempt to discern your counterpart's limitations.
- ❑ Set minimum and maximum boundaries for your agreement.
- ❑ Determine the relative importance of each of your goals.

Deciding on an Approach

Regardless of what approach you ultimately select, it is almost always in your interest to be as flexible as possible, and to take a neutral negotiating stance at the outset.

- ❑ Tailor your approach to the specific situation at hand.
- ❑ If one approach fails, try another.
- ❑ Maximize alternatives and options.
- ❑ Keep your counterpart's interests in mind.
- ❑ Be firm, but sincere.

Chapter Six

Paths to Agreement

To do all the talking and not be willing to listen is a form of greed.

Democritus of Abdera

Establishing areas of mutual agreement can be an excellent way of putting aside the issues that often sidetrack a negotiation. It has been my experience that there are usually many areas of mutual interest between the parties.

After both sides have presented their positions, the first thing you should do is locate these areas of mutual agreement. You can then concentrate your efforts on the goals, interests, and proposals that you don't agree on. Addressing and mediating areas of disagreement will be treated in depth in the following chapters.

Working through areas of agreement is a terrific way to create goodwill between two parties. As you progress through the various areas of agreement and find goals that you share with the other party, you cannot help but feel good about the cooperative and relationship-building positive resolution of these potential conflicts.

As an extra benefit, while you work through these areas of agreement you will start generating momentum to carry you through the areas of disagreement that you will face later on. You can then tap the store of goodwill that you developed early on in the negotiation, and apply it to help get through the difficult issues that lie ahead.

As we explore the development of mutual objectives, you will learn how to identify and develop the interests that you share with the other party, and how to use the concession of your own interests to catalyze the negotiation process. We will also examine the topic of bargaining for mutual agreement, and discuss the philosophy of concluding an agreement quickly, if at all possible.

DEFINING SHARED GOALS

All parties to a negotiation should have the same ultimate goal. That goal is to reach a mutually beneficial outcome that will make everyone who participates a winner.

By establishing mutual objectives early in the negotiation process, the entire mechanism can often be accelerated. While you may disagree on certain specific points, you may discover that you both want to reach the same endpoint or outcome.

In the following case, we will see how early establishment of mutual objectives can help facilitate the ultimate negotiation of an agreement between a manager and an employee.

As manager of new product development, Martika has been assigned the task of bringing three new products to market before the end of the company fiscal year. The projects are behind schedule, and it seems clear to Martika that she is going to have to ask her employees to start working overtime to catch up.

Since summer is coming, she knows it will be difficult for her employees to forestall their vacation plans and take time away from their families to work on this project. But knowing how important this project is to the company, she feels strongly that the employees should make the sacrifice to help ensure their company's future viability.

* * * * *

"As you know, Jim, we have been working on the new geographic information system project for the better part of this year. We are falling way behind in our schedules. The due date for this project is March 31st. We absolutely cannot be late. Thank you for your efforts so far—you've done a great job. We've got to do something drastic, however, to get this project back on track."

"I'm not sure what we can do at this point, Martika. We've already put a lot of extra time into this project. It's just a matter of not having enough hours in the day to get everything done."

"That's exactly what I need to talk to you about, Jim. I'm going to need your help, and the entire team's help, now more than ever. Starting this weekend, I would like you to work at least a half day on Saturday. Then, starting the following week, I would like you to put in at least two extra hours each evening. I know that this is going to be an imposition on you, but this project is absolutely crucial to our company's ultimate success. I'm really going to need your help on this."

"I'm just not sure if I can swing that or not, Martika. By the end of my regular shift, I'm pretty well beat."

"I knew before I asked you that it would be difficult. The company's primary goal, however, is to grow revenues 20 percent this next year. If we can't get these products out, we're not going to get anywhere near that goal.

"Jim, how do you feel about our company's mission? Do you share the same goals I do—to ensure the health of this company, and make sure it is a viable operation that will continue to grow and employ more people in the future?"

"When you put it that way, Martika, I certainly do share the same goals. I have been with this outfit for 10 years—I've seen it grow from a garage-shop operation into a $100 million+ company. I've been personally involved in a lot of that growth, and I definitely want to see us continue to grow in the future."

"I am glad to hear that, Jim. I am personally willing to make sacrifices to get the job done. When it's necessary, I'm willing to pitch in and do whatever has to be done to finish the job. I would not ask you to do anything that I wasn't willing to do myself. I hope I can count on your support."

"Sure, Martika. I'll be glad to help out. If there is anything else I can do to help, just let me know."

"Thanks for your support, Jim."

* * * * *

In this negotiation, Martika established a mutual objective that was used to overcome the objections of her employee. Martika and Jim found common ground in the mutual objective of company growth.

A key mutual objective should be the fostering of long-term business relationships. This is clearly a major goal in almost every business situation, whether it involves a supervisor and employee, salesman and customer, or management and union. It is often difficult to cultivate satisfactory relationships with business associates, and long-term relationships are a relatively scarce and precious commodity in business today.

It's much easier to maintain a good relationship than it is to continually initiate new relationships. The objective of maintaining a good relationship can be very important. In fact, the parties may be willing to be very flexible with each other and concede issues which they normally would not consider in order to maintain a relationship that has developed over a long period of time. Employers may be more generous with their long-term employees, and long-term vendors may be more responsive to your needs.

If you're a typical businessperson, you probably have relatively few long-term relationships. Employees who stay with a company long enough to receive their five-year pins are rare. It is, of course, long-term relationships—the kind that we have with our friends, family, co-workers, and other business associates—that we value the most.

While certain short-term relationships may be a routine part of your business environment, undoubtedly the ones that have the greatest value are the ones that have lasted the longest. How many of your friends from high school do you still keep in touch with? Or from college? Or perhaps from early in your career? If you do keep in touch with any of these friends or co-workers from your past, it's likely that you count these relationships among your most cherished.

AGREE TO AGREE

Once you have established the objectives that you have in common with your counterpart, the next step is to agree on those issues, and put them behind you.

It's always best to start a negotiation by reaching agreement on as many issues as possible. Not only are they the easiest to negotiate, but in putting the issues behind you, you'll be able to concentrate your energies on the key obstacles to agreement. By agreeing to agree, you will build a momentum that will begin to snowball and help carry you through the more difficult areas still to be resolved.

The organization I belong to spends in excess of $150,000 per year for printing services. While most of our printing needs are routine, we can always count on a crisis or two to keep things interesting.

On Tuesday of last week, for example, the mayor decided that she wanted a complete copy of the fiscal year 1994 budget on her desk by 11 A.M. Monday morning. Until she made her request, the budget staff was working towards a fairly relaxed deadline several weeks in the future. Our finance department literally worked around the clock, and finally completed the document late Sunday evening.

The only way that we could get the budget printed and bound in time to meet the deadline would be to drop the camera-ready copy off at the printers when they opened Monday morning at 8 A.M..

* * * * *

"You're a lifesaver, Paul. You know how important it is to get this budget to the mayor on time."

"Sure—no problem, Pamela. We've always tried to do the best we could for you over the years."

"Thank you. I guess we had better talk specifics so you can get to work. Okay, the first thing is that we will need 100 copies of the budget. The camera-ready copy is one-sided, but I want you to print it two-sided."

"So far, so good, Pamela. We can take care of that for you. Have you considered how you want the cover and binding done?"

"No, I really haven't. Do you have any suggestions? I just want to make sure that it looks polished."

"I would suggest you go with a perfect-bound document. It's going to cost a little more than, say, a comb-bound or stapled document, but it will look a lot more professional."

"Price isn't an issue with me, Paul. My hot button right now is making sure the budget is on the mayor's desk by 11 A.M. As long as the binding doesn't cause a problem with meeting that deadline, I say let's go with the perfect-bound documents."

"Good. What color would you like us to do the covers in?"

"Let's try a royal blue cover. Do you have that in stock?"

"You're in luck. I just picked up two cases of royal blue card stock last week. We've got you covered."

"So, Paul, you're absolutely, positively certain that you can meet our deadline?"

"No problem, Pamela. You can pick them up at 10:15."

"Well, that's a surprise. I was certain it would take longer than that for you to have them proofed and delivered to us."

"Considering that you're such a good customer of ours, we are willing to make the extra effort at no extra charge to get those budgets to you before the deadline."

"You've got a deal. Let's go ahead and discuss the rest of the terms of this agreement and get you started as soon as possible."

* * * * *

In your day-to-day negotiations, I am sure you have discovered that, in many cases, you and your counterparts share many of the same goals. It then becomes a simple matter of fine-tuning the goals to the satisfaction of both parties.

In the above case, Pamela was pleasantly surprised to find out not only that the printer was willing to meet the 11 A.M. deadline, but he was also able to beat that schedule by 45 minutes. This cemented the agreement. It also pointed out the fact that negotiations don't have to concentrate on conflict. It is generally the case that both parties share the same goals. By simply agreeing to agree, many potential disagreements can be resolved positively early in the negotiating process.

We are all trying, through a cooperative process, to create an environment for the achievement of our goals. Instead of focusing on the conflict that you may fear, focus instead on the mutual goals that you both share.

LETTING GO OF YOUR DREAMS

One very effective negotiation technique is to create and then give away your "dream" goals. We have already discussed the three major classifications of goals: primary, secondary, and dream. Dream goals can and *should* be used as tools to help you draw the primary and secondary interests of you and your counterpart closer together.

Let's use an example to show how this might work. You are in a weekly staff meeting, and your manager announces that she is planning to lay off several workers in your department. The following lists illustrates possible primary, secondary, and dream goals for negotiation with your manager.

Primary Goals

❑ No layoffs in accounting.

❑ Keep department secretary.

❑ Maintain training budget.

❑ Purchase computer upgrade.

Secondary Goals

❑ Minimize layoffs in the purchasing section.

❑ Maintain control of offices that are vacated in the department.

❑ Maintain control over excess office equipment.

Dream Goals

❑ Continue plans for holiday party.

❑ Maintain current staffing of 10 clerical employees.

❑ Continue independence of internal audit staff.

With these goals in mind, let's see how you might handle the use of dream goals to help achieve and maintain the primary and secondary goals that you have decided are truly important to you.

* * * * *

"Have you had enough time to think about our staff meeting this morning, Bob?"

"I was absolutely shocked to hear about the upcoming layoffs, Tanya. I understand that the company is facing more pressure from our competitors, but I didn't think it would come to this."

"You know, I've taken a look at your staff, Bob, and I have some suggestions for you to consider."

"Okay—I'm not sure that I will agree with everything I hear, but let's hear it nonetheless."

"To begin, I've taken a really close look at your organization, and I believe you're a little top-heavy in the payroll section. We can probably make some cuts in your budget for computer equipment, and I want to take a close look at your clerical staff. Also, I really feel that we'll need to double up some of your offices. This would free up some space for the marketing department."

"Wow, that's a big hit! It's hard enough keeping up with all of our payroll changes and paycheck distribution, much less the flexible benefits program and everything else that we have to cover with our current staffing. How are we supposed to make these staffing cuts and still maintain any kind of quality? And you want us to double up, Tanya? Don't you think that business should turn around within the next six months or so? It doesn't make sense to me to give up those offices and, six months later, staff back up and have to find new offices in which to put my employees. I won't be able to manage my staff effectively if we have to split them up!"

"What would you suggest, Bob?"

"If we must go with the layoffs, I might consider downsizing our accounts payable section. There's probably a little bit of fat in that area—we could certainly survive some cuts there. I suppose I could live without all 10 clerical employees. Maybe we could cut a couple of clerical positions, and ask the remaining staff to accept a temporary pay freeze. I know that the company needs to cut its budget, but we need to allow for the computer upgrades we planned for this year. As you recall, these upgrades will make us much more efficient, and perhaps let us get past these layoffs."

"All good points, Bob. What do you think about cutting the accounts receivable staff?"

"I could probably absorb some hits there, but just don't mess with the payroll section!"

"Okay, Bob, let's work up a plan to make some cuts to accounts payable and, maybe, accounts receivable. Also, take a look at that clerical situation and decide if we can lighten up there, too. Regardless of what you say, we've got to decrease the non-labor budget. Given the choice, I would much rather cut computers than people. Once the layoffs are complete, we can review the space allocations and make adjustments as necessary."

"Hey, Tanya. I know where we can save some money without cutting into my computer budget. We should cancel the big holiday party we're planning, and use the money for the computer upgrade. Spending money on a party this year would probably send the wrong message to our employees."

"That's a good point. Let me think about this for awhile—maybe we'll be able to afford the computer upgrade after all."

* * * * *

The above example shows the effective use of dream goals. In this case, the big company holiday party—a dream goal for Bob—was used to help offset his request for continued funding of his computer upgrade.

Always go into a negotiation with as many alternatives as possible. Dream goals, given away at the right time and place, can be a key to achieving your primary and secondary goals.

If you want to be a winner, and if you want your counterpart to be a winner, too, then you have got to develop and utilize dream goals. When you give up one of your goals to the other party, he will feel that you are negotiating in good faith. When *you* negotiate in good faith, the other party will feel an obligation to reciprocate and give you something in return. If you have worked out the timing of your concessions correctly, you should achieve the goals you are seeking in return.

If, on the other hand, you *haven't* been flexible in the bargaining process, the other party will feel cheated.

Have alternatives available. Be flexible. Be willing to give up some of your goals in exchange for your counterpart achieving some of her goals. As you concede your dream goals, the other party will gain something from the negotiation and will be more favorably disposed to its final outcome.

BARGAINING

Bargaining is the essence— the *raison d'etre*—of negotiation. And not just bargaining for a lower price. Bargaining can, and should, be used in all of your everyday business interactions or tasks. The next time an employee asks you for some time off, see if you don't feel just a little like a State Department diplomat as you negotiate.

Each of us moves a little closer to our objectives as we bargain. We make offers and counteroffers, and we counter counteroffers until we eventually reach an agreement.

Quid pro quo is the name of the game. Giving something to get something in return. It is a concept as old as human existence. It's not just a business technique—it's a part of human nature. As long as we are fortunate enough to be residents of this planet we call Earth, *quid pro quo* will still make the world go round. Sure, the concepts will be rediscovered by eager writers and seminar trainers in the future. The time-worn concept of good-faith negotiating will be dusted off, recycled, and relabeled with faddish new names.

The basic concepts remain the same, new labels notwithstanding. It all comes down to the golden rule. Do unto others as you would have them do unto you.

WRAP IT UP!

Now is a good time to try to conclude the negotiation, if possible. The momentum that has been building as you explore and agree on your mutual interest can carry you through to a rapid conclusion. With only a few remaining areas of disagreement, you may be able to make quick compromises and wrap a final agreement.

It's clearly in your interest to push for an immediate conclusion, if at all possible. After you have nailed down your areas of mutual agreement, mention the remaining areas of disagreement, almost as an afterthought, and suggest a quick resolution to them.

This technique can be used quite effectively once you recognize that you have reached this point in the negotiation process. You want to get your counterpart to overlook the obstacles that stand between you and your final objective. You don't have to apply undue pressure to your partner. Instead, apply the momentum that you have generated thus far in the negotiation to carry you through to a final agreement.

Always present your positions to the other party in such a way that agreement can be reached quickly on the critical issues. The remaining areas of disagreement can be downplayed and resolved without extensive deliberation. It is far better to reach agreement quickly than to invest in the uncertainty, time, and expense of a protracted negotiation.

WORKSHEETS

More often than not, we share many of the same goals with our counterparts. When we work through areas of mutual agreement with another party, we can't help but generate goodwill as a natural result of the process. The negotiation of areas of agreement also tends to sustain this goodwill through the rockier negotiation of mutual disagreements.

Defining Shared Goals

Since the discussion and negotiation of mutual agreements can be so beneficial to the ultimate outcome of your efforts, the following steps should always be close to the top of your agenda:

❏ Establish mutual objectives with your counterpart.
❏ Refer to your mutual objective of a long-term relationship.
❏ Avoid solutions that guarantee short-term relationships.

Agree to Agree

Once you have identified your areas of mutual agreement, formalize your agreements and move on to other issues.

❏ Recognize and agree to your mutual objectives; then put them behind you.
❏ Identify and attack the key obstacles to agreement.
❏ Use your momentum to help propel you through areas of disagreement.
❏ Emphasize cooperation over conflict.

Letting Go of Your Dreams

Dream goals can be used to achieve your major goals and objectives. The more dream goals you have at your disposal, the more flexible you can be as you negotiate an agreement.

- ❏ Review your primary, secondary, and dream goals.
- ❏ Use your dream goals to achieve your primary and secondary goals.
- ❏ Prepare as many dream goals as possible.
- ❏ Give something of value in exchange for receiving something of value.

Bargaining

Bargaining is the essence of negotiation. Whenever you offer a concession, make sure you receive one in return. Always be fair, and refuse to be taken advantage of.

- ❏ *Quid pro quo*—give something to get something in return.
- ❏ Do unto others as you would have them do unto you.

Wrap It Up!

If at all possible, try to complete your negotiation at this point in the process. In this manner, you can best take advantage of the goodwill that you have developed with your counterpart.

- ❏ Use mutual agreement to facilitate a rapid conclusion to the negotiation.
- ❏ Don't pressure your counterpart to finish the negotiation.
- ❏ Emphasize areas of agreement; downplay remaining areas of disagreement.

Chapter Seven

Defusing Disagreement

Drinking together in the evening we are human.
When dawn comes, animals
We rise up against each other.

Antimedon

We've tried everything described in the previous chapters. We've established our goals, set our limits, and researched our topics. We've prepared our rationale, and met with our counterparts. We've explored and agreed on our mutual interests and objectives. We have even traded away all of our dream goals. But we still can't reach a mutually agreeable solution. Now what?

The real art of negotiation is in turning disagreement into agreement . . . of becoming a verbal alchemist by turning your partner's "no" into "yes." The most difficult task for any negotiator—whether amateur or professional—is to negotiate areas of disagreement.

Understand that you will not always reach agreement on every point. There *will* be times when there is no obvious solution. If that is the case, then be prepared to walk away from the impasse and carry on with your life. Don't waste your time trying to resuscitate a negotiation that lost its pulse long ago. But don't give up too soon. There *is* a systematic method to isolate and attack each area of disagreement and bring it to resolution.

RECOGNIZING AREAS OF DISAGREEMENT

To quickly resolve disagreement, you first have to identify the root areas of disagreement. The proposal and counterproposal process will surface disagreements that cannot be resolved. Note these areas of disagreement as they come up, and be prepared to study and discuss them further.

The following example will illustrate a technique for identifying and confirming areas of disagreement.

John and Chuck both work for a major pharmaceutical firm. John, the director of human resources, is in charge of policies that relate to all employees. Chuck, the operations manager of the company, is ultimately in charge of all the employees in the plant's production department.

Recently, concerns about potential safety problems caused by drug and alcohol abuse have been voiced by management. In response to these concerns, the human resources department has suggested that new policies be developed and implemented to allow testing of production employees for drug and alcohol abuse. John and Chuck are negotiating the implementation of these policies with an eye towards how they might affect individual employees. Their joint recommendation will be presented to senior management for final discussion and execution.

                          *   *   *   *   *

"I've read through your new drug and alcohol abuse policy, and I have a few questions about it. What I want to do first, though, is understand exactly what the major goals are. Do you have a few minutes to discuss this?"

"Of course, Chuck, I'll be glad to. This is going to affect your employees more than anyone else's. I want to make sure that you can live with these policies. You're their boss—I don't want to do anything to jeopardize your relationship with your employees."

"Thanks, John. I do have a few concerns that we need to address. This policy has to be fair to all employees. We want to improve plant safety, but we have to protect the rights of our employees. Can you run through the key points of the new policy with me?"

"To begin, this policy would apply to every employee who is in a safety-sensitive position—not just production employees. Each employee in this work category will be tested on a random basis for a variety of drugs and alcohol. I have proposed that these tests be conducted randomly, but that each employee be tested at least four times a year. Once a particular employee has been tested, he or she would not be tested again until the following quarter."

"Wait a minute, John. Don't you think that's overkill? It's going to be hard enough as it is to get this policy off the ground with my guys. Once or twice a year seems like plenty of testing to me."

"I don't agree, Chuck, but let's continue. When an employee has been selected for testing, I would suggest that the plant security guard escort him or her from the plant floor directly to the plant health unit. There, our nurse will administer the test."

"Wait, John. It's going to be embarrassing to my employees to be escorted by plant security. I think we ought to have the employee's supervisor do the escorting."

"No, I don't agree with you on that one either, Chuck. We need to make sure the employee is escorted by an independent third party who isn't biased in favor of the employee. Anyway, upon administration of the test, the sample will be labeled and sent to an independent lab for analysis. Once we get the results of the test back, we will meet with the supervisor to discuss those results. If the results are positive, the employee will be subject to our new disciplinary policy. If the results are negative, the employee's supervisor will be notified and, of course, the employee will also be notified that he has passed the test."

"So how are we going to handle employees who test positive?"

"That is something that has concerned me. I want to make sure that this is a fair policy, keeping in mind that it's critical that we have a safe workplace. The new disciplinary policy is, admittedly, a stern one—it has to be. When the employee fails to pass the test, the employee will be notified, as well as the employee's supervisor. We will ask the employee to pack up his or her personal belongings, and then have plant security escort the employee from the building."

"That's not fair, John. Employees should have the opportunity for rehabilitation. The least we can do is direct an employee who doesn't pass into our Employee Assistance Program. If they make it through EAP, we should let them back into the organization. Anyone can make a mistake."

"I don't know, Chuck. I don't want us to come across as being soft on this drug and alcohol issue. You know we've got a problem. Let's go through the policy one more time. I want to see exactly where we agree and where we disagree."

"All right, let's do it."

"We both agree that there's a need for a drug and alcohol policy here at the plant—right? Can we agree that we are both concerned about the safety of individuals at the plant, and that not only are the individuals who are working in an unsafe manner endangered, but also innocent bystanders?"

"Sure, I agree with that, John."

"Now, we don't seem to agree on the following points. While I feel that random testing four times a year should be instituted for each employee, you feel that once or twice a year is sufficient."

"Correct."

"Furthermore, I believe that once an employee is selected for testing, he should be escorted to our health unit by the plant security guard. The testing will be conducted by the plant nurse immediately. You have stated that you think employees should be escorted by their supervisors."

"Right."

"Finally, I have proposed that, if an employee fails the test, we terminate him. You have suggested that an employee get two chances."

"Let me interrupt you there, John. You may have misunderstood what I said. I actually said that an employee should be referred to the Employee Assistance Program before we terminate him."

"Right, Chuck. I must have misunderstood you. Your idea is that employees would have a second chance to pass the test, after attending a rehabilitation program. If the employee does not pass the test the first time, he or she would be referred to the Employee Assistance Program."

"Correct."

* * * * *

In the above situation, a negotiation is taking place between parties who have both a personal and business interest in the topic. The first player is the human resources manager. He is interested in minimizing risk to employees, property, and product in the pharmaceutical plant. The operations manager, on the other hand, while agreeing with the policy in an overall sense, has to work with the individual foremen, supervisors, and employees on a day-to-day basis.

While the discussions aren't very contentious, the two parties have identified their respective areas of disagreement. The human resources manager, John, has restated the key points, thus bringing them to the surface and confirming their understanding. While this may seem to be intuitively obvious, many people forget to verbally confirm each detail before they proceed.

RANKING THE ISSUES

Once you have identified the areas of disagreement, rank the issues in their order of importance. Do this on a marker board or a large sheet of paper so they can remain visible while each is being discussed. Not every area of disagreement is going to be as important as another.

By ranking these areas of disagreement, you can both clarify and prioritize them. This will help you determine which areas should be focused on, and which areas can be potentially discarded during the negotiation process.

I have found it beneficial to rank-order areas of disagreement on a marker board. If you meet with your team members in a conference room, you can discuss the areas of disagreement, and then write them on the marker board. You might want to brainstorm to get as many areas of disagreement out into the open as possible.

You might find it especially helpful to divide these issues into the three major categories that we developed earlier (with the exception of the last, which has been re-titled for this purpose): primary, secondary, and inconsequential. The example below is taken from the discussion regarding implementation of drug and alcohol testing at the pharmaceutical plant.

Primary Disagreements

1. Frequency of testing.
2. Who will escort employees to the test.
3. Termination ground rules.

Secondary Disagreements

1. Referral to Employee Assistance Program.
2. Number of chances to pass the test.
3. Cost of administering the program.

Inconsequential Disagreements

1. Which company analyzes the tests.
2. Random versus announced testing.
3. Date the testing starts.

ASSESSING VALUE

While the value of an issue may be difficult to quantify, it is true that you will be more or less willing to negotiate away an item depending on what you expect to get in return. An area of disagreement does not have any intrinsic value in and of itself. It only has value relative to the other items that can be traded in return. Value is subjective and is determined by each party during the course of the negotiation. The issues will have totally different values placed on them by different individuals.

What, for example, would you be willing to give up if your opponent decided that he or she would be willing to cut the price in half? Similarly, if you decided to give your employee a 10 percent raise, what would you expect to get in return? All issues have value, and only through your determination of that worth can you begin to get a sense of what you are willing to concede during the course of a negotiation.

Value can be expressed in many different ways. Value can be your cost of time lost, or it could be the pressure of an accelerated schedule. It could represent goodwill you have earned in the process, enhanced performance by your employees, or the ability to work more closely with your supervisor. All of these items have values not necessarily expressed in terms of dollars and cents.

COMPROMISE SOLUTION

Disagreements are resolved by the give-and-take process. Of course, this doesn't mean that the other party does all the giving and you do all the taking! The give-and-take process has to be a balanced and cooperative effort. Don't fool yourself into thinking that you can win through intimidation, or by being the biggest shark swimming in the ocean. To be a real winner, you have to make your counterpart a winner, too. It's just that simple.

In my previous incarnation as director of administration for a software development firm, employment agreements were a very hot topic, particularly in regard to the protection of our proprietary information and the very real possibility that an employee might leave the company and compete directly against us.

The following situation was not uncommon. Note the interplay of both participants in this typical give-and-take negotiation.

* * * * *

"Before I sign this agreement, we need to resolve a few issues. Some of these terms are too restrictive and, frankly, seem quite unfair to me."

"Well, Steve, I'm not sure what you find objectionable about it. The company has spent a considerable amount of time and money in the development and legal review of this agreement."

"That may be true, Roger, but we're going to have to satisfactorily resolve these problems before I'll sign. Three points are particularly objectionable to me.

"The clause that restricts me from joining a company that is a direct competitor of this company for a period of five years after I terminate employment seems patently unfair. I can understand your firm's concern about someone stealing company data and using it to compete unfairly. I can assure you, however, that I would never consider doing anything like that.

"I'm also having a hard time with the clause in the contract that requires me to agree that I can be fired at any time for no specific reason.

"Finally, as far as I can tell, this agreement would be in effect for the rest of my life. Clearly, in any agreement of this nature, there should be some specific termination date established. I feel the agreement should only be in effect as long as I am an employee with this company."

"Okay, Steve, let's address your concerns one by one. Your first objection, the clause which does not allow you to compete against us for the next five years, is something that our company won't budge on. Employees have taken our proprietary information in the past and then used it to compete directly against us. The concern about this kind of situation comes all the way from the board of directors.

"Let's address your second area of concern, the right to terminate without cause. That particular clause is there at the insistence of our legal department. I'm sure you are aware of some of the large judgments awarded against companies for wrongful termination."

"Sure."

"While I positively believe that we have never wrongfully terminated anyone, Steve, our lawyers insist that we protect ourselves from this type of litigation. This is a standard clause which gives us that protection. I don't feel that it unfairly jeopardizes your rights in a termination situation.

"As far as your third area of concern goes, I can understand your apprehension as to the open-endedness of the agreement. We may be able to make some form of concession in that area. Perhaps we could establish a term that is reasonable and does have some definite termination date attached to it."

"What I propose we do, Roger, is revise these three areas. I would like to suggest some alternative solutions to these problems. While I understand the company's concerns, and I definitely want to do everything I can to comply with your requirements, I do have to look out for myself in these matters."

"All right, Steve, why don't you go ahead and I'll look at your suggestions."

"Thanks Roger. I will be willing to sign a proprietary information agreement which prohibits me from taking any information from this company and transmitting it to anyone else without the company's permission. I personally feel that you should be able to rely on my word and, in fact, my written promise that I will not do this. It seems unfair to me to have this as a part of my employment agreement. A separate proprietary information agreement would be suitable in this case.

"As for my second area of concern, I may be able to be flexible here if we can reach some form of agreement on the other two issues. While I am not saying that I am to that point yet, I will consider, depending on how the rest of the agreement works out, easing up in this area.

"Finally, I feel that the agreement should only be in effect as long as I am an employee of this company. I don't see any reason why it should go on any longer than that. Once I terminate my relationship with this company, this agreement should also terminate."

*   *   *   *   *

Steve and Roger will continue to negotiate in this give-and-take fashion until a final agreement has been reached. The parties to the negotiation will defend the goals they feel most strongly about, and give up positions they feel less strongly about, until a final agreement can be reached.

BRAINSTORMING

You may find that there are issues that you still cannot resolve. What are you going to do next? The best solution is to brainstorm alternatives for resolution.

Have you considered every possible aspect of the factors peripheral to the agreement? There's a very good chance that, in your initial look at the different issues, some were overlooked. Take a closer look at the parameters of the agreement and try to find every tool possible to convert areas of disagreement into areas of agreement. Let's see how to use this technique to generate more alternatives to resolve an impasse.

When my wife and I purchased our home five years ago, our best offer was, not surprisingly, somewhat less than the sellers found acceptable at the time. After several weeks of back-and-forth negotiation, we still had not been able to get past our last few areas of disagreement.

* * * * *

"This is really disappointing, Peter. We've been at it for three weeks now, and we're still $10,000 apart. If you think about $10,000, amortized over a 30-year period, it's really an insignificant difference."

"I'm sorry, Andy, but $10,000 is $10,000 in my book. Jan and I really love the house—it's in a great location and it would be perfect to raise a family—but we've already moved far enough. We can't go any farther."

Jan and I were married only a few months earlier. We knew that the condominium we lived in near the beach wouldn't be big enough to contain the family that we were planning to start soon. The location was great, just two blocks from the ocean, and the views were inspiring, but 1,200 square feet was just too small.

In 1988, the Southern California housing market was booming. The pool of willing buyers far outnumbered the sellers. Most buyers assumed that the market would continue its steep upward climb well into the future. Why wouldn't it? Life was good. These facts combined to make most sellers very inflexible in their negotiating positions.

Andy, our real estate agent, had brought over the latest counteroffer from the sellers. It appeared that we would never be able to bring our respective positions into conjunction. While we were willing to pay a premium for the house because of its size and location near Kate Sessions Park, the house did not have a garage, some of the wiring was suspect, and the roof needed repair before the rainy season started.

On the other hand, the sellers, who originally bought the house for $40,000, were looking forward to maximizing the cash that they would be able to take with them into retirement. Our agent, Andy, suggested that we try one last-ditch effort to find a compromise that would meet the needs of all the parties. Andy met at the office of the seller's real estate agent, Karla, to discuss the deal one more time.

"Karla, perhaps we should try to brainstorm some alternatives to break this deadlock," suggested Andy. "We're only $10,000 apart—there must be something we can come up with. I know the Economys are serious about buying the house, and I am certain that the Jacksons are serious about selling. This can still be a winning situation for everyone involved."

"You're right, Andy. Let's give it everything we've got!"

"I have spoken to the Economys, and they told me that they have some concerns regarding repairs they will have to make after they take possession. As I mentioned to you last week, the property inspection disclosed that the roof is way beyond its useful life. The inspectors also discovered evidence of termite damage, as well as inside wiring that does not appear to have been done to code."

"So what are you suggesting, Andy?"

"What I am suggesting is that the Jacksons should consider crediting the Economys for the needed repairs. This would significantly narrow the difference between the parties."

"I can certainly ask them to consider it. Here's another possible solution, Andy. As you know, the Jacksons originally listed their property with the explicit understanding that the appliances, rugs, and furniture would not convey to the buyer."

"Right."

"Well, it turns out that the property that the Jacksons are going to be moving into is considerably smaller than their present residence. They are now interested in selling the refrigerator, washer, dryer, the family room furniture, and the patio furniture."

"That should be a big help. The Economys are living in a condominium right now. They don't have much in the way of furniture or appliances. I think they have one of those compact stack-unit washer-and-dryer setups. They definitely don't have any patio furniture. Do you have any idea how much the Jacksons want for their items?"

"No, Andy, I don't. I'm sure I can get a complete price list together pretty quickly, though."

"That's great, Karla. Maybe we can get everyone to agree to some credits based on the repairs and the appliances and furniture. After that's all said and done, we should be close enough."

"And if we're still not quite there, I would be willing to take a little less commission, if it means that we get the deal. What do you think, Andy? Are you with me on this?"

"Definitely! Half of my commission is a whole lot better than nothing. Let's present these ideas to our clients and see if we can't get this deal back on the right track!"

* * * * *

Andy and Karla have completed a process of brain-storming possible alternatives to resolve their disagreements and produce new pathways to agreement. Armed with these additional alternatives, the parties now have many more opportunities to reach a final agreement.

As you can see from this example, it's important for both parties to participate in this process. If only one party throws out ideas, it is probable that those ideas will be perceived to be one-sided by the other participant. Never let a couple of issues of disagreement become stumbling blocks to a final agreement. Before you give up on a negotiation, make sure you have explored every possible alternative to reaching an agreement.

TAKE TIME . . . GIVE TIME

It's absolutely critical that you give yourself plenty of time to work through an agreement. When parties are rushed or feel pressured to reach agreement, 9 times out of 10 at least one of the parties will get a losing deal. Be patient. Be on your guard. Refuse to be drawn into time traps.

Instead, take the time to work through an agreement. Take time to present your proposal point by point, and to make sure that you have effectively communicated your message. Conversely, you should allow the other party time to communicate his proposals and rationale.

If you feel you need more time to consider a proposal, just say so. If the other party needs to slow down, feel free to give him more time to think things over. Maintaining flexibility is the best guarantee that you have to reach a fair and reasonable agreement.

You may sometimes find that the best course of action is to suspend negotiations for some period of time. If you can break a negotiation off and then return to it later, you will undoubtedly find yourself better able to think through and thoroughly organize your thoughts. Sometimes a good night's sleep can work wonders in giving you new perspectives.

Here are a few ways to suggest that negotiations be temporarily suspended:

"What do you think about taking a break for a few minutes? I'm going to have to take some time to think about what we just discussed."

"I'm supposed to be in a staff meeting in five minutes. What if we break now and get back together tomorrow morning?"

"I've had it! Let me take another look at this later. I'll have my secretary set up an appointment—probably in the next week or two."

WORKSHEETS

The most difficult task for any negotiator is to convert areas of disagreement into areas of agreement. The key to defusing disagreement is to systematically address each individual disagreement, and bring it to a mutually agreeable resolution.

Recognizing Areas of Disagreement

To negotiate areas of disagreement, you have to be able to recognize them. Note these areas as they come up, and be prepared to address them with your counterpart.

- ❑ Identify the root areas of disagreement.
- ❑ Take note of disagreements as they surface.
- ❑ Be prepared to study and discuss the areas of disagreement.
- ❑ Restate and confirm your understanding of the areas of disagreement.

Ranking the Issues

Just as you can attach different levels of importance to each of your goals, so, too, can you assign a relative value to the disagreements that you share with the other party.

- ❑ Rank the areas of disagreement.
- ❑ Clarify and prioritize disagreements.
- ❑ Discuss the areas of disagreement with your counterpart.
- ❑ Determine which areas of disagreement should be concentrated on.
- ❑ Divide disagreements into primary, secondary, and inconsequential.

Assessing Value

To ensure that you keep all the issues in perspective, it is important to examine their value relative to other issues.

- ❑ Determine the value of each issue relative to all other issues.
- ❑ Disagreements do not have intrinsic value.
- ❑ Value can be expressed in many ways besides dollars and cents.

Compromise Solution

The easiest and best way to resolve areas of disagreement is through a balanced and cooperative effort with your counterpart. Winning through intimidation, or through the application of other pressure tactics, is short-sighted, at best.

- ❑ Disagreements are resolved through a cooperative process.
- ❑ To be a winner, make your counterpart a winner, too.
- ❑ Be flexible.

Brainstorming

Flexibility in resolving a disagreement is directly related to the ability to generate alternatives that are acceptable to both parties.

- ❑ Consider every possible aspect of the factors peripheral to the agreement.
- ❑ Convert areas of disagreement into areas of agreement.
- ❑ Ensure that both parties participate in generating alternatives.

Take Time . . . Give Time

Negotiations subject to time or other pressures can easily have win-lose outcomes. Even if you have to suspend negotiations for a period of time, it is better to do so than to be pushed into an agreement that doesn't fulfill your goals.

❑ Refuse to be drawn into time traps.

❑ Don't rush or pressure your counterpart into an agreement.

❑ Take the time to present and receive proposals.

❑ If necessary, suspend negotiations until they can be revisited.

Chapter Eight

When Deadlock Occurs

The shoe that fits one person pinches another; there is no recipe for living that suits all cases.

Carl Gustav Jung

Not all negotiations end in agreement. Many end in deadlock. Deadlock is when the parties to a negotiation have gone as far as they are willing to go, and refuse to move any farther toward agreement.

Deadlock can be avoided through the application of several basic techniques. Keep talking. Use new perspectives in the negotiation. Make a tactical withdrawal. Take a break. Substitute negotiators.

If the deadlock cannot be broken, you may have to go up the chain of command, or negotiate indirectly through a neutral person. You will need to consider alternatives to negotiating and, eventually, you may be forced to abandon the negotiation altogether.

KEEP TALKING

There is clear value in continuing communication while stuck in a deadlock, even if both sides appear to be unwilling to budge from their respective positions. By keeping communication channels open, the potential for eventual agreement is kept alive. The following techniques can keep you communicating when a negotiation has deadlocked:

Metacommunicate. Talk about the fact that communication has broken down. Gain a commitment to continue discussion as a priority. Seek suggestions for continuing to communicate such as: new ways of examining differences between positions; methods of segmenting larger areas of disagreement into smaller points for discussion; or the discussion of scenarios for resolving differences that still exist.

Backtrack. When disagreements become significant, revisit topics that were previously agreed upon. For clarity, and as a review, restate terms and conditions that have been agreed upon, and expand upon details of fulfillment of those terms and conditions. This tactic will reinforce goodwill. It also implicitly assumes that an agreement will eventually be reached.

Sidestep. Discuss issues that are likely to be of secondary importance to the negotiation, such as available options, scheduling details, installation plans, etc. Alternately, focus on minor points of disagreement that can be easily resolved. Low-priority goals are particularly useful. This technique will allow both sides to move closer to an agreement, even though one or more significant differences still remain.

NEW PERSPECTIVES

You can often break a deadlock by approaching the negotiation from a new perspective. A mutually acceptable new method of examining relative positions can serve as a starting point for further compromise. It also keeps you talking with your counterpart.

Introducing a new perspective forces the other person to consider a different, and possibly unfamiliar, alternative. This shift in thought can help to move the topic away from an inflexible position, thus allowing for further discussion and eventual compromise. Perhaps this progress will not lead directly to an agreement, but the effort will continue in a positive direction.

Choose a perspective that will lead you to your goals, and try to get the other individual to agree with the perspective before he can see where it leads. For example, "If we were to offer a compromise that gives you a higher profit, would that be acceptable to you?"

Techniques that can shift your counterpart's perspective include the use of logic, objectivity, acceptability, and analysis:

Logic. Logic is a universally acceptable basis for progressing in a negotiation, especially when combined with undisputed facts regarding the situation. "Why should I give you a raise if I can bring in a temporary at half the cost?" Here, one party is attempting to make the other person see his factual perspective.

Objectivity. Impartial criteria or examples can help a person consider other perspectives and options. "Let's look at the industry average and see how your sick-leave rate compares," or "Here are the standard benefits offered by our competitors; as you can see, our benefits package includes them all." In these cases, you are requiring the other person to consider another perspective based upon additional facts.

Acceptability. This technique goes beyond the current impasse to some point in the future. It seeks to define the other person's goals. "What can I offer to get you to say 'yes' to these terms today?"

Analysis.   New means of analysis can add dimensions to a negotiation. Suggest other methods of analyzing the issues that are being negotiated. "We've been arguing about numbers without regard to the value of quality. Let me show you how the quality of our product will save you money over the long haul."

Granted, with a stubborn opponent, these techniques may not move negotiations out of a deadlock, but they are worth trying, and the attempt to do so will indicate a continued willingness on your part to reach an agreement.

WITHDRAWING YOUR OFFER

When we can't have something, we often want that thing even more. This human trait can often be used to unlock deadlocked deliberations. In business, the threat of withdrawal is often accomplished by making a conditional offer. The offer generally contains an explicit condition for revocation, usually by way of a specified time limit.

While I generally advise against the use of any tactic that could be perceived as exerting pressure against your counterpart, many businesspeople will just not respond unless they have a deadline. The possibility of the withdrawal of an offer can be a very useful way to test the sincerity of your counterpart.

If he really wants what you have to offer, your counterpart will respond positively to your deadline. Conversely, if the threat of withdrawal does not result in a reasonable response from the other side, it's a clear indication that the other individual is either trying to bluff, or he is not that interested in what you have to offer. Business is fraught with examples of this technique.

"If we don't make substantial progress on these demands by midnight, we'll have to call for a general strike."

"If I don't get that raise by this month, you better start looking for someone else to run the store!"

"This special once-a-year sale ends at midnight tonight!"

The threat of withdrawal can be a very effective way of breaking a deadlock, if it is used sparingly. If overused, the other side will soon see through your artifice. It's best to use this tactic only in the most trying of circumstances.

SUBSTITUTIONS

When negotiations deadlock, interpersonal relationships may also deteriorate. Individuals may find it increasingly difficult to deal with each other as tensions mount. Feelings of animosity and bitterness are often inevitable.

In such cases, the substitution of individuals on one or both sides of the negotiation can be a highly successful strategy. When you hear one of the following statements from your counterpart, it may be time to substitute negotiators:

"You're being unfair and unreasonable. If you can't be more businesslike in your dealings, then we'll never get anywhere."

"It seems our personalities are getting in the way of our discussion."

"I couldn't care less, at this point, if we reach an agreement or not."

Simply bringing in a new negotiator can be a highly effective technique for breaking deadlocks. A substitute can feign ignorance of previous problems, and enter the negotiation with a fresh perspective. Since the new negotiator was not a party to the earlier, contentious debate, he won't carry any emotional baggage into the discussion. As emotional issues are pushed to the side, deadlock will break and progress can continue.

If you initially came across poorly and negotiations break down, you can substitute a team member who may have developed a better rapport with your opponent to resume communication.

GOING OVER THEIR HEADS

It's very frustrating to find out that your counterpart either doesn't have the authority, or is afraid to take the responsibility, for making a decision. This kind of problem, which can occur at any level in the organization, is found most commonly when individuals are negotiating together for the first time.

The person you are dealing with may not be the individual with authority to make the decision. He or she may simply be collecting information and passing it on to someone else to review and decide.

Alternatively, the individual may have the responsibility to make decisions, but be afraid to make the necessary commitment to close a deal. This may be because he or she is new to the position and unclear about his or her objectives, or unsure about what procedures are considered acceptable by the organization. Whatever the case, if you want to be successful, immediate action must be taken.

If negotiations have been broken down due to the lack of authority, it is necessary to identify the true decision-maker and bring him or her into the process. This, of course, is much easier said than done, but identification of the person with the authority is essential. The sooner you find the right person, the sooner you can complete the negotiation.

Once the true decision-maker is identified, you must be especially careful in handling your counterpart. Be diplomatic. Remember that your goal is to find solutions that address the interests of both parties. Avoid statements that may provoke your counterpart, such as the following:

"This is a big waste of my time! Let me speak to your supervisor—now!"

"You obviously don't know what you're doing. Let me talk to someone who does."

"If you can't make a decision, let me talk to someone who can!"

It is much better to get to a real decision-maker by including your counterpart in all discussions. This can be accomplished without threatening the individual if your tone, attitude, and word selection is appropriate:

"Can we both sit down together with your district manager and work out some options?"

A person with decision-making authority who is afraid to exercise that authority can be a formidable roadblock to the negotiation process. Once again, it is critical to take action against the impasse. As in the previous example, it may be necessary to go over your counterpart's head to obtain your goals. Remember, though, that your long-term business relationships require that such actions be handled in a diplomatic manner.

These situations will be easier to resolve if you have established some amount of rapport with the other individual. The existence of rapport indicates the development of trust between you and the other person.

Trust is a crucial element in establishing and developing effective negotiating relationships. Trust makes sensitive interpersonal maneuvers, such as the ones we've described in this section, much easier to accomplish.

INDIRECT DISCUSSIONS

If negotiations have broken down and you are not speaking to your counterpart because talking is further alienating you both, you can still communicate indirectly through a neutral third party. Communicating indirectly allows you to test possible compromises without risk and without losing face. Since offers or concessions are communicated indirectly, the principals can distance themselves from the process and, instead, concentrate on the content of the message.

A common approach in large-scale negotiations is the use of the news media to convey changes in one side's position to the other side. Of course, this technique is not appropriate for the vast majority of daily business negotiations.

An approach that is often just as effective, and certainly much more easily carried out, is the use of a neutral third party. Such individuals can often be more objective since their involvement is limited. An agent's predominant interest and motivation can be solely to help both sides reach a mutually agreeable compromise.

Another advantage of using an intermediary is that he can lend credibility to your positions. For example: "I know Mark and, if he says this is the best deal he can get approved, he means it;" or "I've never known Margaret to be late on a delivery even though it's not specifically required in her contract; she's committed to excellence."

CREATING ALTERNATIVES

Even if communication has come to a grinding halt, you can still make progress towards your objectives. Examine your goals and determine who else can fulfill them. In business, this often means going back to survey the market. Increasing your options in this manner will significantly strengthen your negotiating position.

Perhaps your counterpart will hear of your new efforts (you could even tell her), and she might, as a result, be more inclined to reinitiate negotiations with you.

Another alternative is to suspend negotiations for a specified period of time. This technique is similar to taking a break, but is specifically used when negotiations are deadlocked. Time can change the value of any offer and, after an appropriate period, one or both of you are likely to be more eager to come to an agreement.

GIVING UP

Often, your willingness to walk away from a deal will give you greater leverage in obtaining a reasonable and mutually acceptable agreement. Reexamine your position and ask: "Do I really want to agree to these terms? Is there any flexibility or room for compromise in either of our positions that I have not considered? What are the consequences if this negotiation does not end in agreement?"

If you can't agree to agree, leave an option open for future communication. At all costs, avoid burning any bridges. You never know when you'll need to negotiate some other topic with the same person again. Successful and confident businesspeople make every effort to avoid holding grudges. Instead, they simply chalk up a failed negotiation to experience.

WORKSHEETS

Recognize that not all negotiations will end in an agreement. Occasionally, due to reasons that may or may not be within the control of the parties, negotiations become deadlocked. When deadlock occurs, it is critical that immediate action be taken to get discussions back on track.

Keep Talking

If you aren't talking, you aren't communicating. If you aren't communicating, you'll never break a deadlock. The following techniques can help you keep the channels of communication open:

- ❑ Metacommunicate.
- ❑ Backtrack.
- ❑ Sidestep.

New Perspectives

When you are stuck on a point, it often helps to bring in a fresh perspective. This is where having alternatives can be a great asset. Use:

- ❑ Logic.
- ❑ Objectivity.
- ❑ Acceptability.
- ❑ Analysis.

Withdrawing Your Offer

While pressure techniques should generally be avoided, it is sometimes necessary to threaten to withdraw your offer if substantive progress towards your goals is not being made.

❏ The threat of withdrawal can be a very effective way to break a deadlock.
❏ Conditional offers take the form of explicit conditions of revocation.

Substitutions

When personalities clash, as they often do in heated negotiations, it is often beneficial to bring in a new individual.

❏ Deadlocks often cause a deterioration of interpersonal relationships.
❏ Substitute negotiators can break deadlocks by defusing emotional issues.

Going Over Their Heads

If your counterpart cannot make a commitment, or refuses to make a commitment, you may have to go over his head. Due to the sensitivity of this option, this technique has to be used sparingly, if at all.

❏ When your counterpart cannot make a commitment, take immediate action.
❏ Identify the real decision-maker and bring him into the process.
❏ Be diplomatic.

Indirect Discussions

When none of the other techniques work, it may be necessary to communicate indirectly.

❏ You can communicate indirectly without risk and without losing face.

❏ You can accomplish your goals through the use of neutral third parties.

❏ The intermediary can lend credibility to your positions.

Creating Alternatives

As always, the more alternatives you have at your disposal, the higher the probability that you will achieve your goals. If you can't reach agreement with the current party, be prepared to find someone else you can reach agreement with.

❏ Examine your goals and determine who else can fulfill them.

❏ Perform a market survey.

❏ Suspend negotiations for an agreed-upon period of time.

Giving Up

Some agreements were not meant to be. If, after you have explored every possible option and alternative, you still cannot reach agreement, then move on.

❏ Reexamine your position.

❏ Leave options open for future communication.

❏ If negotiations remain deadlocked, chalk it up to experience.

Chapter Nine

Wrapping It Up

No grand idea was ever born in a conference, but a lot of foolish ideas have died there.

F. Scott Fitzgerald

Closing is probably the most critical part of the negotiation process. Without a successful outcome, it is not enough to have gone through all the different techniques described in this book. A negotiation can be fumbled just as easily, perhaps even more easily, at closing as it can anytime earlier in the process.

There are several different techniques you can use to facilitate a successful closing. In the final analysis, it is important to create an environment in which your counterpart will be able to say "yes." Once you have nailed down an agreement on a particular issue, it is important to confirm this agreement, preferably in writing.

Close the negotiation on an up note, and find ways to reinforce the goodwill that has been developed during the process. If, despite your efforts, you still can't bring the other party to successful closure, find ways to move on and defuse any animosity that may have developed.

MAXIMIZE ALTERNATIVES AND OPTIONS

The ultimate goal in the negotiation process is to have both parties arrive at a mutually satisfying arrangement.

You may consider it an oversimplification, but this is why you have invested all of the work and preparation and discussion with the other party. Until you both say "yes," you cannot close a negotiation—regardless of how much both of you want to do so.

So . . . how do you both agree to agree? You have already seen that both parties must attain some, if not all, of their goals. You must create an atmosphere of flexibility within which you and the other party can maneuver. Only through flexibility will you be able to find innovative ways to achieve your goals.

If you approach a negotiation with an inflexible agenda, you will find that it is very difficult to bring the other party to successful closure. Instead, the other party will resist your efforts at reaching compromise and will balk at reaching a final agreement.

Compromise is the solution. Both parties must be prepared to give a little to reach a final agreement. You each have to recognize that it is in your mutual interest to give a little to get a lot.

Before you give up on negotiation, try every option and alternative possible to reach an acceptable final outcome. If you are truly interested in wrapping up the agreement, and the other party is, too, you will be able to find compromises that, while perhaps outside of your original range of consideration, are now within the range. Make it easy for the other party to say "yes." At the same time, make sure that when *you* say "yes," you have assessed your own goals and can ensure that they are being met.

Performance appraisals are probably one of the least-favorite tasks of any supervisor or manager. As important as it is to take the time to formally tell our employees how they are doing, performance appraisals always seem to end up at the bottom of our lists of priorities.

One of my field supervisors, Pamela Langshaw, was preparing to discuss the performance appraisal of one of her employees with me. Pamela was very pleased with her employee's performance and wanted to make sure that he was given significant recognition. Pamela was also aware that business had been down over the past few quarters, and that management was considering the implementation of financial austerity measures.

Pamela and I met to discuss the appraisal over lunch at a nearby restaurant.

* * * * *

"Peter, I'm sure you're aware that Greg is a very productive member of our project staff."

"Yes, Pamela, I have heard a lot of good things about Greg. Wasn't it Greg who received that letter of commendation from our customer?"

"That was Greg. We would have overrun the project if he hadn't been able to make those revisions to the plan in response to the changes in our customer's schedules. Not only were we able to respond to the schedule changes, but we were able to reduce our expenses at the same time."

"Too bad we don't have more employees like Greg. So what's the bottom line, Pamela?"

"There's been a definite improvement in Greg's performance over the past year. He has always been a good performer, but this year I believe he made some very outstanding contributions."

"I know about the project plan revisions. What else has he done that you consider to be outstanding?"

"Greg played a large part in the River City project. In fact, he almost lived in the office while we were working on the proposal. There's no way that we would have made the due date without his help."

"All right, Pamela. It sounds like Greg has done a fine job. So what do you recommend?"

"I have put a lot of thought into this. I would like you to authorize a 10 percent pay increase for Greg. While this might seem high, I strongly believe that his performance merits it."

"I'm sorry, but 10 percent is out of the question. I know that Greg is doing a great job but, considering the losses that we have recently experienced, we need to cut, not increase, our labor expenses."

"I know we're having financial difficulties. If it weren't for the outstanding contributions of employees like Greg, however, we would be in even worse shape. We've got to reward high performers in good times as well as bad. Otherwise, we'll lose them to our competitors."

"Pamela, company management has set a limit on salary increases. That limit it 5 percent. I can't authorize an increase in excess of that number, no matter how indispensable the employee is."

"There's got to be something we can do. What is the status on the incentive bonus pool—has it been cut?"

"As far as I know, it's still intact. What have you got in mind?"

"Would you agree that, if the company's situation were better, we would be able to agree to the full 10 percent increase for Greg?"

"I suppose so, Pamela. Greg's performance has been outstanding over the past year."

"What if we make up the difference between 5 and 10 percent with a cash bonus? It's my understanding that the funds in the bonus pool are derived from last year's profits and are therefore unaffected by our current losses. If I can confirm that the funds are available, would you agree to the cash bonus?"

"Sure, Pamela. I'll look into it when we get back to the office."

* * * * *

As the above example shows, Pamela knew how to use the power of alternatives to achieve her goals. What's more, Pamela knew her supervisor well enough to know what kinds of alternatives she should present to him. Instead of letting the corporate-mandated limitation on salary increases get in her way, Pamela found an alternative which would make it relatively easy for me to say "yes."

Assuming that the bonus pool was intact, Pamela would be successful in reaching her goals. Even if a bonus was out of the question, you can bet that Pamela would have other options available for me to consider. By anticipating the possible objections of her supervisor, and by having alternatives available for her supervisor to consider, Pamela virtually guaranteed that she would reach her objective.

Learn to anticipate the goals and objections of your counterpart. If you can present a well-thought-out option that meets every objection that your counterpart voices, you will eventually achieve your goals. Not being prepared with alternatives only increases the probability that you will not overcome your partner's objections and will therefore be unable to close the negotiation.

Instead of creating reasons for your partner to say "no," build mutually satisfying opportunities for him to say "yes."

CONGRATULATIONS—
NOW, CONFIRM IT!

Congratulations! You've reached agreement with your counterpart! Now that your agreement is complete, it is vital that you confirm it. Sometimes we're all so delighted to have completed the major parts of a negotiation that we fail to notice that there are items yet to be agreed upon.

By confirming your agreement before you terminate your meeting, you can be assured that all the pieces of the puzzle are defined and properly set in their places.

You may be familiar with the children's game called "telephone." To play this game, you and your friends sit in a circle. The bigger the circle, the more entertaining are the outcomes of this game. One player will tell a story to the person sitting next to him. Then each person in succession tells the story until it has come around to the final person in the circle. Needless to say, by the time the tale works its way around the circle, the resultant plot has changed dramatically from the original story.

Similarly, the parties in a negotiation may misunderstand or misconstrue what they are agreeing to. Only by confirming the terms of agreement can you be absolutely sure that you are in agreement with the other party, and that your job is complete.

In the following example, I delegated a task to Anna, my administrative analyst. This task, which involved development of a new project sales report, was relatively complex. Note how I obtained confirmation of the task before Anna initiated her task.

* * * * *

"Let's make sure that we fully understand each other on this assignment, Anna. While it's important that the task be completed quickly, it's even more important that the results be accurate."

"Sure, Peter."

"Okay—the summary report will cover the most recent quarter and will concentrate solely on our sales to our commercial customers."

"Right, that's my understanding. Didn't you say that you also want to see the data by month?"

"That's correct, Anna. I am going to need the monthly subtotals to present to my boss, and also to double-check the quarterly totals."

"That sounds like the way to go."

"Why don't you make a note of this, Anna. I want to make sure that there is no confusion over this assignment. Oh, yeah, one other thing . . . I will only need totals on projects in excess of $10,000."

"Okay—I've written it down—let me confirm my understanding. You would like to get the numbers for the most recent quarter as well as the backup for each month in the quarter. We are also going to limit our report to commercial projects over $10,000."

"Right. I'll need the report by the close of business Monday. We need the numbers to support planning for our next budget cycle. Any further questions, Anna?"

"No. I'll start on this right away."

* * * * *

I didn't just delegate the report to Anna and then walk away. Before sending Anna off to do the work, I made sure that she confirmed our agreement. Every point that I considered to be of importance was double-checked to make sure that Anna fully understood the task. Anna restated the goals of the project to me so that I could confirm her understanding.

Always confirm your agreements to ensure that all of your outstanding issues have been successfully resolved. If you're going to find out that you really haven't reached agreement with your counterpart, it's much better to find out before performance begins than to find out later when you are waiting for results.

If you do discover that there are misunderstandings, clarify them with the other party. If the misunderstandings are serious enough, you may have to reopen negotiations to be able to reach final agreement.

Regardless of the outcome, make a habit of confirming your agreements. Not only will you have the peace of mind knowing that you have communicated your goals effectively, but the other party also will feel more secure in knowing exactly what your expectations are.

WRITTEN CONFIRMATION

Depending on the importance or complexity of your agreement, a verbal restatement of the terms may not be enough. If there is any concern on your part that you need more than a verbal agreement, get it in writing.

Some agreements are simple, such as the time you set to meet with an employee to discuss a discipline problem. This agreement does not require written confirmation (although you may desire it for the record). The agreements reached during an employee meeting of this type, however, will surely require written confirmation. Very rarely are verbal understandings good enough in situations related to discipline or other personnel matters. By their nature, written understandings become formal understandings.

Finally, a written confirmation of your agreement may well be the only documentation of the final agreement. The confirmation of agreement, especially if you have the other party sign the document in acknowledgment, becomes a mutually binding, written contract. In the absence of written confirmation, it would be difficult to prove that the other party had not fulfilled his end of the bargain.

Written confirmation can be as simple as a quick memo, or as complex as a full-blown, formal contract. Ultimately, the form of an agreement is not as important as the simple act of getting an agreement confirmed in writing.

I strongly believe that, if the agreement you seek is of sufficient importance, you should always seek written acknowledgement. While you can include words such as, "If I do not hear back from you within one week, I will assume that this agreement is in force," or other words to that effect, it is much better to obtain written acknowledgement from the other party by way of their signature of acceptance to the terms and conditions of the agreement.

Without a written acknowledgement, you may wrongly assume that the other party has received your written confirmation, or has agreed to all terms and conditions, when, in fact, he does not. Letters *do* occasionally get lost in the mail. To be absolutely sure of your agreement, get written acknowledgement of your confirmation. All it takes is a signature line at the bottom for the other party to sign, acknowledging that they have read and agree to the terms you have stated.

SURPRISE, SURPRISE

Isn't it always the case that, just when you think everything is going great, something happens to upset your tidy little applecart? Unfortunately for us, Murphy's Law is often a very real companion in our everyday business dealings. Unintentional surprises are to be expected from time to time. They are merely a reflection of life's unpredictability, and can be easily surmounted.

Intentional surprises, or sneak attacks, however, can be a maddening and frustrating outcome in the negotiation process. Sneak attacks can easily fell the fragile bridges of trust spanning the chasms of uncertainty between business negotiators, taking agreements crashing along with them.

Unintentional surprises can happen at any time and for no apparent reason. They are unpredictable and generally outside of the control of the participants. While the surprise factor can be unnerving to you, it may unnerve your counterpart just as much.

What typically happens is that something unexpected throws an agreement off of its foundations. One or more of the fundamental assumptions of the participants changes, shifting the pattern of the developing agreement to new, unconsidered planes of thought. Any of the following events could unintentionally derail an agreement:

- ❑ Change in department priorities.
- ❑ Denial of funding.
- ❑ Board reconsideration of approval.
- ❑ Participant resignation or reassignment.
- ❑ Change in responsibilities.
- ❑ Corporate bankruptcy filing.
- ❑ Major plant layoff or closure.

There are many, many other possibilities when it comes to unintentional surprises. Knowing that the other party is as surprised as you are may help you pick up the pieces of your shattered agreement and find other ways of reaching your goals.

You may find, especially if your counterpart is embarrassed by or feels guilty about the derailing event, that he will stretch even farther to reach an accommodation with you. Similarly, given a new set of baseline assumptions, you may find that your goals have changed, and that you can be even more flexible in finding a common ground of mutually agreeable solutions with your partner.

Intentional surprises, on the other hand, are premeditated and calculated to elicit a specific reaction from you. They are designed precisely to throw you off balance just as you are wrapping up the last few details of an agreement. If you are not prepared for this tactic, the entire agreement may be thrown into complete disarray.

Fortunately, most businesspeople realize that the use of such tactics is counterproductive to the establishment of long-term business relationships. It only takes one experience with a person who employs this technique to quickly and permanently remove his or her name from your Rolodex or telephone speed-dial button.

The following example illustrates the use of the element of intentional surprise to throw an opponent off balance, and to disrupt the course of a negotiation in favor of the party who has initiated the sneak attack.

Cara and Joseph are congratulating each other over completing a complicated stock transfer between their companies. Negotiations went on for several weeks and were quite acrimonious at times. Agreement has finally been reached, and Cara and Joseph are jubilant.

* * * * *

"That was quite a negotiation, Cara. Thank God it's over!"

"I agree, Joseph. I didn't think we were ever going to get everything wrapped up. Let's sign the final paperwork and go on with our lives. I'll draft the agreement right now and we can sign it within the hour."

"Fine, Cara. I guess there's something that I should let you know first, though. I'm not authorized to sign the agreement. It has to be reviewed and signed by the CEO."

"What? You didn't tell me that! The reason I was able to compromise on the price was because you told me that we were going to be able to sign this agreement today. You didn't tell me that it was going to take any longer than that to get this agreement ratified!"

"I could have sworn that I mentioned that I would have to run this up through management, Cara."

"You absolutely did not, Joseph! This has really got me upset. As far as I'm concerned, the deal is off!"

"Cara, I don't know why this should be a problem. All I'm saying is that we've got to run the agreement past management for approval. It will only take a week—probably less. Is that really a problem?"

"You bet it is. We agreed to execute the agreement today and make the stock transfer immediately. In a week's time, who knows what the value of the stock will be?"

"That's a good point, Cara. In a week's time, the stock may be worth less than it is today. I'm sure you've heard the rumors that a huge second-quarter loss will be announced on Friday. You know, you're right. We should reopen the negotiations. As far as I'm concerned, I think we're paying too much for that stock."

* * * * *

Joseph has intentionally thrown the negotiation off track. He has sprung a sneak attack on Cara, who thought the negotiation was complete. To her surprise, Cara found out that not only was the negotiation not complete, but she was farther away from her goals than ever.

In a case like this, you have to give serious thought to whether or not you want to continue discussions with the other party, or perhaps just walk away. In some cases, you may have no choice but to continue discussions. If you can't walk away, then be absolutely sure that everything that you have agreed to is confirmed, preferably in writing, and that all understandings are on the table for consideration.

If, however, you have the option of walking away from the deal, by all means do so. By continuing to negotiate, you are only rewarding and further reinforcing the negative behavior of your opponent.

People who think nothing of using sneak-attack tactics are not unlike schoolyard bullies who will persist in their art until someone has the courage to stand up to them. Find the courage to tell your opponent to take a hike, even if it means that you have to develop a new source or pay a higher price. In the long run, it will be worth your peace of mind.

The basis for win-win negotiation is trust. Intentional surprises destroy trust. I personally find it very difficult to trust any individual who can not honor his or her promises. Neither should you.

GETTING ON WITH YOUR LIFE

If you can't bring your negotiation to a mutually agreeable close, at some point you'll need to get on with your life. If your negotiation was successfully concluded, go ahead and execute your agreements. If, for some reason, the negotiations were derailed, then don't dwell on their lack of resolution. Instead, move forward and prepare for your next negotiation. Hopefully, you will have learned something from even the most disastrous fiasco that will benefit you in future negotiations.

Sometimes, no matter how hard you try to bring them about, agreements are just not meant to be. Perhaps the ranges of the participants' goals were just too far apart and could not be brought into conjunction. Maybe one party backed out at the last minute. Or maybe your goals were a little too ambitious.

Whatever the case, don't lose too much sleep about it. In business, you will have a countless variety of opportunities to be challenged and to be successful. Take the time, however, to analyze why the negotiation failed. How would you handle the situation next time? Should you scale your goals back, or allow for more flexibility in your positions? Were you dealing with the right person? You may find that you need to make some adjustments to your approach before you try again.

WORKSHEETS

Closing a negotiation is an art unto itself. If you can't bring a negotiation to successful closure, then you will not be able to achieve your goals. The following checklists will help you to close your negotiations effectively and successfully.

Maximize Alternatives and Options

You may find that, as you approach the end of a negotiation, you will be called upon to make additional concessions. Be prepared for this eventuality by maximizing your alternatives and options.

- ❏ Create an atmosphere of flexibility.
- ❏ Avoid inflexible agendas.
- ❏ Compromise is the solution.
- ❏ Be willing to give a little to get a lot.
- ❏ Make it easy for your counterpart to say yes.
- ❏ Anticipate the other party's objections.

Congratulations—Now, Confirm It!

Once you have reached an agreement, it is important that you confirm it with the other party, preferably in writing.

- ❏ Confirm the agreement before the negotiation ends.
- ❏ Get the confirmation verbally or in writing.
- ❏ Resolve any misunderstandings and reconfirm.

Written Confirmations

Written confirmation can take various forms, depending on the complexity of the agreement.

- ❑ All agreements should be confirmed in writing.
- ❑ For simple agreements, obtain a letter of confirmation.
- ❑ For complex agreements, insist on a written agreement or contract.

Surprise, Surprise

Occasionally, while you are in the final stages of a negotiation, surprise events can throw progress into a tailspin. Both intentional and unintentional surprises can destroy the progress that you have worked so hard to achieve.

- ❑ Unintentional surprises are outside the control of the participants.
- ❑ Unintentional surprises can happen at any time.
- ❑ Explore other ways of reaching your mutual goals.
- ❑ Intentional surprises are calculated to throw you off balance.
- ❑ Intentional surprises destroy trust.
- ❑ If you have the option of walking away from the deal, exercise it.

Getting On with Your Life

Recognize that not every negotiation will end in a successful outcome. Give it your best shot, but don't accept a bad deal just because you feel compelled to enter into an agreement with the other party.

- ❑ If an agreement can't be reached, don't dwell on it.
- ❑ Some agreements are not meant to be.
- ❑ Turn a failed negotiation into a chance to review your goals.

Chapter Ten

Putting the Basics to Work for You

Nothing will ever be attempted, if all possible objections must first be overcome.

Dr. Samuel Johnson

As men and women in business, we undoubtedly negotiate more often, and under a wider variety of circumstances, than those in any other profession. This being the case, it is therefore critical that all of us in business develop and maintain well-practiced negotiating skills.

If you have gained nothing else from this book, I hope that you have learned that business negotiation should be a cooperative undertaking rather than a competitive one. Negotiations are not contests to see who can exert the most authority over the other party. Remember that the Latin root of the English word negotiate means simply "to carry on business."

To be a successful negotiator, you don't have to be intimidating, overpowering, or aggressive. Instead, you need only possess a strong belief in your ultimate goals and in the practice of cooperative, win-win negotiation skills. The best negotiations by far are those that encourage all participants to become winners.

Successful negotiators have the ability to step back from the personalities and concentrate on the issues. Too often, we let our emotions get in the way of rational business discussions. Leave your emotional baggage at the door and focus on the job at hand. No matter how heated the discussions may get, always treat your counterpart with the very same respect that you would demand for yourself.

Remember that trust and commitment are the basis for the establishment of credibility. Transform your words into action. And never, never back out of your commitments.

Be able to say "no" to the other party. However, if you say "no," make sure that you have options and alternatives to present that address your counterpart's needs and interests. You will get nowhere if you have not given yourself the room and the flexibility to negotiate. Remember that you are negotiating not to argue, but to reach agreement. Flexibility in your goals will allow you to give some of them up to help your counterpart achieve his goals, thus increasing the probability that the other party will also find flexibility in meeting your goals.

Refuse to be rushed into an agreement. Be patient. Take all the time you need to fully explore every factor in an agreement.

Finally, understand that some agreements are never meant to be. If no amount of discussion can bring about a satisfactory agreement, then thank your counterpart for giving it his best, and walk away.

While most of your negotiations should lead to final agreement, there are bound to be a few that are destined to failure. With just a little bit of practice and preparation, I am confident that the skills and techniques in this book will help bring you success every time you negotiate.

Index

1. How did you find out about this Briefcase Book?

- ☐ Bookstore ☐ Irwin Catalog
- ☐ Advertisement ☐ Convention
- ☐ Flyer ☐ Other Catalog
- ☐ Sales Rep
- other _____

2. Was this book provided by your organization or did you purchase this book for yourself?

- ☐ individual purchase
- ☐ organizational purchase

3. Are you using this book as a part of a training program?

- ☐ yes ☐ no

4. Did this book meet your expectations?

- ☐ yes ☐ no

(please explain) _____

_____

_____

_____

5. What other topics would you like to see addressed in this series?

(Please list)

_____

_____

_____

6. ☐ Please have a sales representative call me.

I am interested in:
- ☐ bulk purchase discounts
- ☐ custom publishing

7. ☐ Please send me a catalog of your products.

_____
Name

_____
Title

_____
Organization

_____
Address

_____
City, State, Zip

_____
Phone